THE REPORT OF THE INDEPENDENT COMMISSION ON THE VOTING SYSTEM

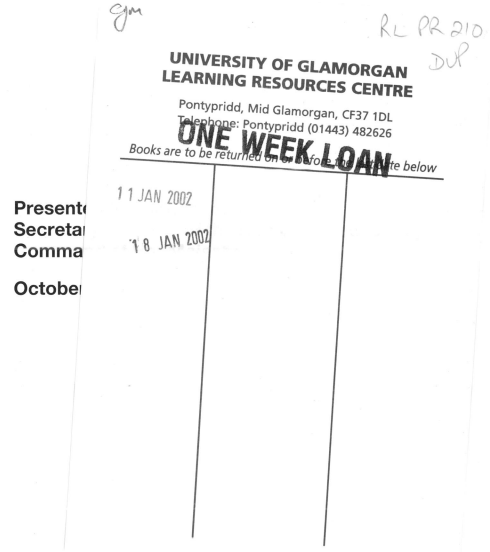

Presente
Secretar
Comma

Octobe

Cm 4090-I

£10.30

THE
INDEPENDENT COMMISSION
ON THE VOTING SYSTEM

The Rt. Hon Lord Jenkins of Hillhead OM (Chairman)
Lord Alexander of Weedon QC
Baroness Gould of Potternewton
Sir John Chilcot GCB
David Lipsey Esq

25 October 1998

Dear Home Secretary,

In December 1997 I was invited to preside over an Independent Commission on the voting system with the remit to recommend an alternative to the existing system for Parliamentary elections to be put before the people in a referendum. I was asked to report within the year. The Commission started its work in January and I am now pleased to enclose our report.

11 870982

Learning Resources
Centre

Yours sincerely,

Roy Jenkins

The Rt Hon Jack Straw, MP
Secretary of State for the Home Department
Home Office
50 Queen Anne's Gate
LONDON
SW1H 9AT

Contents

Terms of Reference and Membership

The Independent Commission on the Voting System was established by the Government in December 1997 with the remit to report within 12 months. The Commission started its work in January of this year with the following terms of reference.

- The Commission shall be free to consider and recommend any appropriate system or combination of systems in recommending an alternative to the present system for Parliamentary elections to be put before the people in the Government's referendum.

- The Commission shall observe the requirement for broad proportionality, the need for stable Government, an extension of voter choice and the maintenance of a link between MPs and geographical constituencies.

There were 20 formal Commission meetings at all of which every member of the Commission was present.

Membership of the Commission

The Rt. Hon Lord Jenkins of Hillhead O.M
Lord Alexander of Weedon QC
Baroness Gould of Potternewton
Sir John Chilcot GCB
David Lipsey Esq

We were exceptionally well served by our team of Home Office officials headed by Rosalind McCool. Gus Park provided fine intellectual stimulus until he had to leave us at the beginning of September. Ragnar Clifford who came to us in June proved an admirable replacement. Rosalind McCool and he worked exceptionally hard in the latter days to enable us to meet the exact target date which we had announced at the beginning of our work. Belinda Kay and Gemma Pearson provided good backup.

Acknowledgements

The Commission is extremely grateful to everyone who has contributed to its work within the UK and overseas. We have received over 1500 written submissions and letters from members of the public, academics, political parties, MPs, and lobby groups. A list of the main contributors is provided at Annex G. Particular thanks goes to David Butler and his fellow academics for their report on a number of technical issues and also to Professor Patrick Dunleavy and Dr Helen Margetts and to Professor John Curtice for the research they conducted on the Commission's behalf.

We would also wish to thank the High Commissioner for New Zealand, Dr Richard Grant and the Ambassador for Germany, Herr Gebhardt von Moltke for their helpful contributions. Special thanks also goes to the British Ambassadors to Ireland and Germany and High Commissioners in New Zealand and Australia for their hospitality during our visits overseas, and to their staff James Tansley, Stephen Smith, Carol Hinchley and Brian Davidson who worked so energetically and successfully on our behalf in preparing for and conducting our programmes. We are grateful to all who gave their time to see us in the course of our visits. A full list of our interlocutors overseas is provided at Annex F.

We are also grateful to Sir John Quinton, Chairman of the Metropolitan Police Committee for graciously allowing us use of his well-appointed room for Commission meetings.

Finally, the way in which we approached our work is described at Annex E.

Chapter One: Introduction

1.   The remit which we were given by the government in December 1997 was to recommend the best alternative 'system or combination of systems' to the existing commonly-called 'First Past the Post' system of election to the Westminster Parliament. In doing this we were asked to take into account four not entirely compatible 'requirements'. They were (1) broad proportionality; (ii) the need for stable government; (iii) an extension of voter choice; and (iv) the maintenance of a link between MPs and geographical constituencies.

2.   Fortunately the 'requirements' were none of them absolute. Otherwise our task would have been not merely difficult (which it certainly has been) but impossible. Proportionality may be 'broad' not strict. 'Stable government' in the context is necessarily a relative term, for the only way to ensure it absolutely (at least until the régime blows up) would be by avoiding elections altogether, which would make our enquiry otiose. Voter choice is at once important and imprecise. And it is 'a link' and not 'the link' between MPs and geographical constituencies which has to be respected. This semi-flexibility has made it possible for us to aim at a point which comes near to reconciling all four criteria.

3.   It must be stressed that there is no question of our being asked to impose a new electoral system upon the British public. What we are asked to do is to recommend the best alternative system which will then be put to the British electorate in a referendum. There has been some suggestion from the opponents of any electoral change (see for instance the House of Commons debate on 2 June 1998) that we should have been given the opportunity to consider the virtues of the present system and to adjudicate between it and all alternatives. But this is surely a misconceived argument for it would have given us a power which we do not have and do not seek. The one proposition which is guaranteed a place upon the referendum ballot paper is the maintenance of the *status quo*. Our rôle is merely to recommend what the alternative should be.

4.   Nevertheless it has in practice been inevitable that when considering the advantages and disadvantages of any new system we should have been constantly measuring them not only against each other, but also against what exists today and in the course of that we necessarily had to deploy arguments both for and against the existing system. It is further the case that none of us are electoral absolutists. We all of us believe that any system has defects as well as virtues. Some systems are nonetheless much better than others, and we have endeavoured to seek relative virtue in an imperfect world.

Chapter Two: The Meaning of Representation

5.   Before we get into the comparison of the merits of different systems we think it right to set out certain assumptions which have lain behind our work. These relate first to our concept of 'fairness' in electoral outcomes; second to the place of political parties; and third to the role of Members of Parliament, who are an important outcome of any electoral system.

Fairness and the Role of Parties

6.   First, 'fairness', which is an important but imprecise concept. Fairness to voters is the first essential. A primary duty of an electoral system is to represent the wishes of the electorate as effectively as possible. The major 'fairness' count against First Past the Post is that it distorts the desires of the voters. That the voters do not get the representation they want is more important than that the parties do not get the seats to which they think they are entitled. Parties should, like the electoral system, be servants rather than masters, although in their case it is necessarily to a segment rather than to the whole which they appeal. If they aspire to be parties of government, however, that segment needs to be a wide one, and if the nation as a whole is to function well they need also to show some respect for the opinions of their opponents. Parties should not elevate themselves into mystical entities, enjoying special rights of their own. That way lies what can be described as the 'tabernacle' approach to politics, by which all virtue lies with those within the sacred temples and all those outside are eternally damned. Such an approach is almost certainly a recipe for parties getting above themselves, being intolerantly dogmatic when they are successful, and degenerating into narrow sects when they are not. It is also a recipe for the 'blame the other side for everything' confrontational style of politics, which has done much to reduce respect for the functioning of the House of Commons and for politicians generally, and which in the quite recent past has also encouraged a confrontational mood in industry, although that is less of a problem today that it was a couple of decades ago.

7.   It is also the case that the near unanimous opinion which was expressed to the Commission in its consultative hearings around the country was a distrust of any electoral system which increased the power of party machines. While we do not deceive ourselves that the limited number who attended these meetings can be regarded as a representative cross-section, this persistent current of opinion, coming as it did from those who were hostile to any change as well as from the committed reformers and some who were more neutral, made a strong impression upon us.

8.   Allowing for this, however, it is important not to be carried too far by a fashionable current and to pretend that representative democracy can function without parties. Within the Commission's own electoral systems context it is impossible not to use the results for parties as the principal criterion for measuring 'unfairness'. The basic evil is unfairness towards voters but its manifestation is unfairness to various groups, of which some (women, ethnic minorities) are not specifically political, but with parties nonetheless being the principal beneficiaries or losers. In saying this we are not unmindful of the argument that, in justifying fairness, what is sometimes called 'proportionality of power', as well as proportionality of representation should be taken into account. Just as the gross and persistent under-representation of a substantial minority cannot be justified, so it would be undesirable to correct that by giving to

the minority such a permanent hold upon hinge power that neither of the larger groupings could ever exercise independent power without the permission of the minority. That would substitute one distortion for another. But a balance can be struck. If in the catch-phrase (and somewhat misleading like all such phrases) we avoid the tail wagging the dog this should and can be done without all dogs having their tails cut off.

9.   Within a wider context it is also the case that any Parliament endeavouring to function without any party organisation would be an inchoate mass, incapable not merely of giving effective sustenance to government (and thus meeting the second of our terms of reference requirement) but even of organising its own business, from electing a Speaker to deciding which issues should be debated on which day. As, in addition, parties are mostly sustained by those with a spirit of public service, we do not see our role as being either on the one hand to denigrate parties or on the other to increase the already very considerable powers which are exercised by these necessary tools of democracy.

The Role of the Members of Parliament

10.   The role of Members of Parliament can now be broadly regarded as four-fold: to represent their constituencies; to provide a pool from which most of the holders of ministerial office are chosen; to shape and enact legislation; and to enable the party in power to sustain the central planks of its legislative programme whilst yet being held to account for its executive action.

11.   The House of Commons fulfils the first two of these distinct but overlapping roles with marked effectiveness. There is no doubt that most of its members work hard in their constituencies and once elected regard themselves as representing the entire electorate within their constituency regardless of which party individual electors supported at the polls. This convention has been rightly valued down the years by almost all MPs. The workload of members within their constituencies has grown, as is illustrated by an explosive increase over the years in the size of their postbags. In contrast to the not so very distant past, members are expected to spend a lot of time in their constituencies. Our clear impression is that most members take this constituency responsibility very seriously and discharge it well. With devolution, this constituency role will not be so obvious for members in Scotland (in particular), Wales and Northern Ireland, since many of the issues a member has traditionally dealt with will be handled at devolved level.

12.   Similarly few governments have not been able to recruit from the House of Commons a ministerial team which contains several stars and maintains a general level of competent and devoted public service. This is not contradicted by the fact that nearly all governments have found it necessary to bring in a few people not previously in Parliament for some ministerial posts. This has become notably so for Law Officers, Scottish ones for some time past, more recently for English ones as well.

13.   By sharp contrast it is difficult to be at all sanguine about the performance of the House of Commons as a legislature. There is a mass of complex legislation each session. The tasks imposed on the relevant civil servants and parliamentary draftsmen are demanding. There is no doubt that in the past much legislation has been hastily conceived, and that imprecise ministerial instruction or sheer pressure of time have resulted in inadequate thought being given to the precise form in which legislation is brought forward. We hope that the increasing trend towards pre-legislative scrutiny will contribute to an improvement in the draft legislation presented to Parliament.

14.   Legislation is not very effectively scrutinised in the House of Commons. In most cases, government MPs are expected to and do support the first and each subsequent versions of a bill equally faithfully. Usually only amendments which are introduced by the Government have much chance of success. The theory that any government always knows best or will assuredly get it right first time is not easy to sustain. Nor does the career structure of parliamentary politicians encourage many backbench MPs to concentrate on the painstaking, low-profile work of improving the quality of legislation. A lot is left for a revising second chamber to do.

15.   Inevitably perhaps, the competing responsibilities of MPs do not assist them in the task of coping with the large and complex burden of legislative business. We believe nonetheless that there is considerable scope for some members to concentrate more fully and more critically on the legislative process and for there to be amongst the mix of members some who have appropriate expertise and temperament to undertake the grinding and often unnoticed slog of improving the quality of our laws. For on those laws depend the legal foundation and economic and social balance of our society.

16.   The fourth, and for many the most central, role of the House of Commons is to ensure that the executive is held fully accountable for its actions. This task is hard when governments elected by minority votes can command large majorities. Fortified by the whipping system, by the natural loyalty to their leader of most MPs and by an equally natural desire on the part of many for political preferment, this can lead to what Lord Hailsham in 1976 memorably described as 'elective dictatorship'. He was speaking during a period of Labour government, which had been supported by only 39% of the electorate, but which was nonetheless pushing through what appears in retrospect at any rate to be some of the last gasps of a dogmatic desire for nationalisation – of the ports and of the aircraft industry.

17.   A decade or so later, however, a Conservative government, with only a few percentage points more of electoral support behind it, pushed through first the disciplined enactment of the poll tax, and then, within the same parliament, its equally disciplined repeal. This was followed in the 1990s, in the last years of a government moving towards heavy electoral defeat, by further measures of privatisation, from the railways to the Stationery Office, of questionable popularity. In view of this record it may be thought that some greater diffusion of power through the encouragement amongst MPs of more independence and more concentration upon the legislative process would be desirable. Insofar as a reformed electoral system could assist in this direction that would be a mark in its favour.

Chapter Three: The Current System

18.   Next we set out what appear to us to be both the qualities and the defects of the existing First Past The Post or simple plurality in single-member constituencies system (henceforth referred to as FPTP; a brief description of this and the other main electoral systems is provided on the inside of the front cover of the report).

The Virtues of FPTP

19.   First the virtues. It is the incumbent system. It is familiar to the public, votes are simple to cast and count, and there is no surging popular agitation for change. It usually (although not invariably) leads to a one-party majority government. It thus enables electors, while nominally voting only for a local representative, in fact to choose the party they wish to form a government. It then leaves each member of Parliament with a direct relationship with a particular geographical area, on a basis of at least nominal equality in the sense that they are all elected in the same way. It also enables the electorate sharply and cleanly to rid itself of a unwanted government.

20.   The case can be expanded in the following ways.

(i)   By giving to all MPs each a unique position in their constituency for the period of their incumbency it encourages them to try to serve all their constituents well, and however partisan members may be at Westminster, to practise a more even-handed approach in their base.

(ii)   The single-party government outcome may be seen as assisting quick decisions – although there are one or two examples to the contrary – and the implementation of a sustained line of policy.

(iii) Where a government fails, or at least disappoints, it can easily be punished by the electorate.

(iv)   By its 'winner takes all' and 'loser (particularly second or third losers) gets very little' effect it encourages parties to broaden their appeal and thus discourages extremism. (It can also be said, however, that in certain circumstances it encourages extremists to infiltrate moderate parties because the system gives them so little to gain on their own.)

(v)   It offers to unorthodox MPs a degree of independence from excessive party control, provided (as many of them do) that they can retain the support of their local organisation.

Historical and Political Context

21.   These are by no means negligible virtues, partly springing out of and partly providing the reasons why the system has persisted for a long time in Britain (although not, in exactly its present form, as long as is widely thought). There are one or two glosses which need to be put upon this list of virtues before more fundamental criticisms are considered. First the single member constituency is not an inherent part of the British parliamentary tradition. It was unusual until 1885, and only became the rule in 1950. Until the first date most seats were two-member, one (the City of London) four-member, supplemented by thirteen three-member ones in the large cities. These last were created by Disraeli's 1867 Reform Act, each

elector having only two votes, the limitation introduced with the deliberate intention of providing for minority representation. Until 1950 a number of two-member boroughs persisted, in which it had been often the case that the two members were not of the same party; this was indeed the way in which most members of the early Labour party, frequently in double harness with a Liberal, secured their entry into Parliament. There were also the twelve university seats, three of which were two-member and one three-member, all of these multiple ones elected on a system of a Single Transferable Vote.

22.   Second the FPTP system, although familiar, certainly could not be said in recent decades to have produced a House of Commons the functioning of which commands strong respect. There has been a long history of attempts to replace or at least substantially to modify the system. Many of these go back well into the nineteenth century. There were two high points of such attempts. First, the 1917 all-party Speaker's Conference which unanimously recommended a switch to a Single Transferable Vote system in the cities and large towns, accompanied by the use of the Alternative Vote in the counties. The various propositions foundered in a series of cross party currents with unfavourable votes in a not very well-attended wartime House of Commons. Then in 1931, under the second Labour government, a bill for the introduction of the Alternative Vote got through the House of Commons, but was rejected by the Lords and was lost with the break-up of that government in the following year.

23.   The third occasion when there was a surge of criticism of FPTP was in the mid 1970s, when, following a perverse general election result in February 1974 (the Conservatives had a lead of 0.7% or 226,000 over Labour, but secured fewer seats, and the Liberals got only 2% of the seats for 19% of the vote), about a hundred Conservative MPs (in step with the CBI resolution of 1977) pronounced themselves in favour of electoral reform, the enthusiasm of many of them fading away during the long period of Conservative power in 1980s. However such fluctuation of view in accordance with changing party need has by no means been peculiar to the Conservatives. The Liberals were indifferent to the issue during their ten years of early twentieth century power, and as late as 1917 the London Liberal Federation even produced a pamphlet entitled *The Case Against Proportional Representation*. The Labour party showed matching hostility in the years from 1945 to 1979 when they enjoyed somewhat more than an equal share of power. The Labour party renewed its interest in the late 1980s which led to the admirable analysis of the Plant Report. There is enough here to prompt the cynical thought that there has been an element of 'The devil was sick, the devil a monk would be, the devil was well, the devil a devil he'd be' about the attitude of all parties to electoral reform. Their desire to improve the electoral system has tended to vary in inverse proportion to their ability to do anything about it.

24.   The Liberal Democrats, in contrast with one side of their early twentieth century ancestry, are of course strongly in favour of electoral reform, and have a great interest in its effect. It is inevitable that when a system has heavily discriminated against a particular party, as FPTP has undoubtedly done against the Liberal Democrats, they are likely to be substantial beneficiaries of a change. But to have an interest in an outcome does not necessarily vitiate advocacy of it. Churchill had a great interest in victory in the Second World War. But that does not mean that the quality of his rallying cry should be dismissed on the ground that 'he

would say that, wouldn't he'. Furthermore the Liberal Democrats are against the simple introduction of the Alternative Vote, despite the fact that it would be of substantial benefit to them.

25.   We are of course aware of the considerations of *realpolitik* which have informed the bigger parties in framing their positions at and since the 1997 General Election. However, the narrow interests of the two parties are by no means obviously reflected in their positions. The Conservative party, which has often done well out of FPTP in the past, although not particularly so in 1992, was hit on the head by it in 1997. Not only were Scotland, Wales and all the big provincial cities (with the solitary exception of the Sutton Coldfield appendage of Birmingham) rendered an absolute electoral desert for them (in spite of their polling an aggregate of 1.8 million votes – or 17% of the total in these areas), but their overall reward of only 25% of the seats for 31% of the vote meant that the rest of the country was not adequately rich in compensating oases. Yet the Conservative evidence to this Commission shows that their faces are now firmly set against any change from the system which has temporarily treated them so harshly. The members of this cross-party Commission wonder, however, how fully the Conservative party has appreciated the longer-term nature of a bias against them which has recently entered the FPTP system and how additionally difficult this will make a quick and major resurrection. This point will be explained when we come to one of the broader deficiencies of FPTP in paragraphs 40–43 below.

26.   The Labour party, *per contra*, has after many thirsty years had a cornucopia of luscious psephological fruit emptied over its head. FPTP, aided by some mutual tactical voting from and to the Liberal Democrats, has rewarded it with 63.6% of the seats for 43.2% of the vote. On a 'what we have we hold' basis 1997–8 might be expected to be the most improbable period for the Labour party leadership to contemplate electoral reform. Yet, perhaps on grounds of wider statesmanship, perhaps with a shrewd instinct that when you have as much as this you are historically very unlikely to hold anything like the whole of it, the Labour government, which is already legislating for a more proportional system for the European Parliament, the Scottish Parliament and the Welsh and London Assemblies, has set up this Commission, with the strong presumption that, if well argued, its recommendations will at least be taken seriously. If this disposition persists this Labour government will have the unique distinction of having broken the spell under which parties when they want to reform do not have the power and when they have the power do not want to reform. As a result of this knot the existing electoral system, in many ways irrational, and, to judge from most opinion polls on the subject, not particularly loved either, has persisted.

The Defects of FPTP

27.   The deficiencies of FPTP are principally the following, many of which derive from a natural tendency of the system to disunite rather than to unite the country. This tendency shows itself in several ways.

28.   FPTP exaggerates movements of opinion, and when they are strong produces mammoth majorities in the House of Commons. Since the war it has done this for Labour in 1945, 1966 (less sweepingly) and 1997, and for the Conservatives in 1959, 1983 and 1987. While there is a

considerable case for some clear cut results, there are also disadvantages to 'landslide' majorities, which do not in general conduce to the effective working of the House of Commons. Landslide majorities, our researches suggest, are regarded with considerable suspicion by the wider public, perhaps more so even than coalitions. It is also the case that recent large majorities (both in 1987 and 1997) have been secured with a smaller percentage of the total vote (42.3% and 43.2% respectively) than in 1945 (48.3%), 1959 (49.4%) and 1966 (47.9%). This is of course largely a function of stronger support for a third party.

29.   The FPTP system is peculiarly bad at allowing this third party support to express itself. Half a century ago, at the great mass plebiscite of 1951, when 82.5% voted and 96.8% of them voted for one of the two big parties, it was a negligible problem. The fact that the 2.5% who voted for the third party achieved an even lower percentage of the seats, barely 1%, was not a serious distortion. Already by 1974, as had been seen, this 2.5% had grown to 19.3% of the vote, but still yielded only 2.2% of the seats. And in 1983 the third party, then known as the Alliance, got 25.4% of the vote and 3.5% of the seats. Even in 1997, when the third party benefited from tactical voting, it still got only 7% of the seats for 16.8% of the vote.

30.   This under-representation of a relatively strong minority party is very much a function of that party's appeal across geographical areas and occupational groups. When a party has a narrow but more intense beam, as with Plaid Cymru but less so for the Scottish Nationalists, its representation, although by no means perfect under the present system, approximates more to its strength. This is perverse, for a party's breadth of appeal is surely a favourable factor from the point of view of national cohesion, and its discouragement a count against an electoral system which heavily under-rewards it.

31.   The same properties of FPTP tend to make it geographically divisive between the two leading parties, even though each of them can from time to time be rewarded by it with a vast jackpot. We have already seen how the 1997 election drove the Conservatives out of even minimal representation in Scotland, Wales and the big provincial cities of England. During the 1980s the Labour party was almost equally excluded from the more rapidly growing and more prosperous southern half of the country. South of a line from the Wash to the Severn estuary and outside London there were, in both 1983 and 1987, only three Labour seats. It was also the case that as a result of both of these elections there was no Labour MP for a predominantly rural English constituency. This, also, is a bifurcation which has recently become increasingly sharp. In 1945, for instance, there were three Labour members for Norfolk county divisions, which were then more rural than they are today. And in 1955 there were, unbelievable as it now seems, eight (out of fifteen) Conservative MPs for Glasgow. Such apartheid in electoral outcome is a heavy count against the system which produces it. It is a new form of Disraeli's two nations.

32.   One thing that FPTP assuredly does not do is to allow the elector to exercise a free choice in both the selection of a constituency representative and the determination of the government of the country. It forces the voter to give priority to one or the other, and the evidence is that in the great majority of cases he or she deems it more important who is Prime Minister than who is member for their local constituency. As a result the choice of which individual is MP

effectively rests not with the electorate but with the selecting body of whichever party is dominant in the area. Unless the electorate is grossly and rarely affronted (as appeared to be the case in the Tatton division of Cheshire at the 1997 election), individual popularity in any broad sense hardly enters into the process at all. This is not an inbred deficiency in all voting systems. Both the Additional Member System (as in Germany, see paragraphs 55–61 below) with its two votes and the Single Transferable Vote in multi-member constituencies (as practised in the Republic of Ireland, see paragraphs 50–54 below) allow the voter to combine influencing the choice of government and expressing a preference between individuals as local representative.

Voter choice and 'Making Votes Count'

33.   The next criticism of FPTP is that it narrows the terrain over which the political battle is fought, and also, in an associated although not an identical point, excludes many voters from ever helping to elect a winning candidate. The essential contest between the two main parties is fought over about a hundred or at most 150 (out of 659) swingable constituencies. Even in a landslide election such as 1997 Conservative vulnerability or Labour hopes did not extend beyond the larger range, and in most elections the range has been even more narrowly confined. This indeed was explicitly recognised by what is regarded on all sides as the exceptionally efficient Labour machine in 1997. They concentrated their resources on what they had identified as the vulnerable hundred with all the clinical precision of the German general staff going for weak points in their 1870 or 1940 advances. Outside the chosen arena voters were deprived of (or spared from) the visits of party leaders, saw few canvassers, and were generally treated (by both sides) as either irrevocably damned or sufficiently saved as to qualify for being taken for granted.

34.   To some extent the challenge of the third party provides an antidote to such complacency, sometimes threatening Labour in what would previously have been regarded as safe inner-city seats, and doing the same to the Conservatives in the far West Country and Wessex. This point can however hardly be called in aid of FPTP, for one of the most salient characteristics of the system is that it makes it as difficult as possible for a third party to win seats and thus does its best to render that threat innocuous.

35.   The semi-corollary of a high proportion of the constituencies being in 'safe-seat' territory is not merely that many voters pass their entire adult lives without ever voting for a winning candidate but that they also do so without any realistic hope of influencing a result. In these circumstances it is perhaps remarkable that general election turnouts remain at or a little above a relatively respectable 70%, well down on the 80% plus of Britain in the early 1950s or of Germany last month, but a little higher than the Republic of Ireland or France and well up on the United States. As the Home Affairs Select Committee has recently argued, we should not be satisfied when 3 in 10 voters (although some of them are disenfranchised by an out-of-date electoral register) fail to use the five-yearly opportunity to influence their choice of government. Nevertheless we do not believe that this problem should be solved by compulsory voting.

36.   Although FPTP is often referred to as a 'majoritarian' system this is an increasing misnomer at the constituency level. To a growing extent it is a 'plurality' rather than a

'majority' system. In the four elections of the 1950s an average of only 86 or 13.5% of MPs were elected without having the support of a majority of those voting in their constituency. In the two elections of the 1990s these figures have risen to an average of 286 or 44%. The change is of course a function of the growth of support for the third party (and the fourth in Scotland and Wales). But as a fundamental weakness of FPTP is that it is inherently ill-at-ease with anything more than a two-party pattern, this can hardly be regarded as an adequate excuse. It is a heavy count against a system which claims the special virtue of each MP being the chosen representative of his or her individual constituency if, in the case of nearly a half of them, more of the electors voted against than for them.

Perverse Results

37.   There is also not merely the regular divergence from a majority but occasionally from a plurality in the country as a whole. The perverse result of the first 1974 election has already been referred to. There was also the arguably equally perverse one of 1951, when the Conservatives, although polling 250,000 less votes than Labour, won a small overall majority of 17 seats and skilfully built 13 years of power on this slender base. The irony of that result for Labour was that in terms of crosses on ballot papers it was their best result ever. Both in absolute numbers and percentage of the votes cast they did better than they had ever done before, or have ever done since – better than in 1945, better than in 1997 – and yet they lost.

38.   It may be said that, if two elections of the fifteen since the war have produced perverse results, that is in itself unfortunate, but it nonetheless means that thirteen have given the victory to the party with more votes than any other and that is on average not at all bad. However risks have to be measured by their consequences and not merely by their incidence. Two rainy days out of fifteen would certainly be an acceptable risk for the planning of a picnic, but an air journey which has two chances out of fifteen of ending in a crash would most certainly not be. Nor, in the days of controversy about the death penalty, would for most people be a two in fifteen chance of hanging the innocent. A false election verdict might be regarded as about halfway between the two categories, which is well short of saying that two distorted results out of fifteen do not matter. Nonetheless, in fairness to FPTP, it should be noted that other electoral systems can also produce occasional irrational results.

Wider Representation

39.   There is some, but not overwhelmingly strong evidence that FPTP is less good at producing parliamentary representation for women and for ethnic minorities than are most more proportional systems. In New Zealand, for example, (which we discuss in more detail at paragraphs 67-73) the proportion of women (30% of MPs there are now women), Maoris and ethnic groups increased dramatically following the introduction of a proportional system. And in Germany where a similar system is used the proportion of women in the Bundestag is 26%. Both are significantly higher even than the current UK figure of 18%, itself a great improvement upon the less than 10% upon which it was stuck for half a century. But the point should be noted without giving it a weight which it cannot bear. We can equally point to examples where a more proportional system has not been so successful in this area. In Ireland, for example, under the Single Transferable Vote rather than an Additional Member system,

women make up only 13.9% of the Dail. We believe that, ultimately, under any system, it is the political parties who are responsible for candidate selection, and the matter is in their hands. Nevertheless, a party which has the will to increase female or minority representation might find it easier to do so under a system involving lists or slates of candidates than it would with a system which makes use exclusively of single-member constituencies.

Bias

40. A more certain, and in this list final, criticism of FPTP is its tendency to develop long periods of systemic bias against one or other of the two main parties. These periods of bias (apart from that against a widely-spread third party) are not necessarily permanent but while they last they are very difficult if not impossible to correct. They are in this respect rather like a little ice age or period of global warming.

41. Bias essentially arises when a given number of votes translates into significantly more seats for one party than for the other. For the post-war period until about 1970, as the graph below illustrates, it ran in favour of the Conservative party and against the Labour party. It was largely a consequence of Labour piling up large unneeded majorities in its heartland seats (of which the old mining constituencies were the most conspicuous examples) while failing to pick up a full share of the key voters in the marginal seats. In the 1970s and the early 1980s there were fluctuations around an approximate equality. In the two elections of the 1990s, however, the bias of 1945–70 has drastically reversed itself. The number of votes achieved by the Conservatives in 1992 was not substantially different from that achieved by Labour in 1997. But the former election yielded the Conservatives only what proved a shaky and erodable majority of 21 (and one over Labour of 65) whereas the latter gave Labour an overall majority of 179 (and one over the Conservatives of 255). The discrepancy arises from a mixture of causes, ranging from the over-representation of Scotland and Wales (from which the Conservatives are now wholly excluded), through some inequality in the size of English constituencies, the Boundary Commission being almost inevitably a bit behind the game, and the impact of the Liberal Democrats being now (much more than in the 1980s) favourable to Labour than to the Conservatives, to the most important but most elusive factor, which is that the lowest percentage polls are in Labour (often inner-city) seats, and that in consequence a given number of Labour votes now produces more seats than the same quantity of Conservative votes.

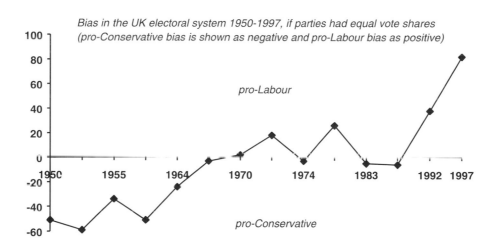

*Bias in the UK electoral system 1950-1997, if parties had equal vote shares
(pro-Conservative bias is shown as negative and pro-Labour bias as positive)*

42.   The combined strength of these factors is such that there is now an almost unanimous psephological opinion that at the last election an equality of nation-wide votes between the two parties would have produced a seat lead of *circa* 76 for Labour, or, put another way round, the Conservatives would have required a lead of approximately 6½% to give them an equality of seats with Labour. In order to obtain an overall majority, taking into account the Liberal Democrats and the Nationalist parties (and the prevalence of such overall majorities and the consequent security of single-party government is the central argument deployed for FPTP) they would have required a very much more substantial lead. While there can be no guarantee that the next election will produce precisely the same level of bias, we can say with some certainty that the system will, for a given level of votes, treat Labour better than it will the Conservatives.

43.   While systemic bias could, on the record, be argued to display a certain impartiality, running for one long period in favour of one party and then for another period in favour of the other, such irrational alternations must be held as a count against the system. It is moreover a bias which could not by definition occur in a fully proportional system and which would be reduced by any significant move in that direction.

Chapter Four: Electoral Systems and Stable Government: Experience of the United Kingdom and Overseas.

44.   The case in favour of FPTP, set out at the beginning, has therefore to be tested against a very substantial list of deficiencies. Apart from its familiarity (which is a point needing to be handled with care, for it can be deployed against any reform of any institution) and its simplicity, the central argument in favour of FPTP appears to be that it alone can produce effective and stable yet democratically elected one-party government, and thus remain true to the best part of the British political tradition.

The British Tradition

45.   The first assumption to be examined in this context is that single-party government is a time-hallowed British tradition. The past 150 years, which began just before Disraeli's celebrated remark that 'England does not love coalitions', an aphorism delivered in a very specifically partisan context but since elevated into a general proposition, gives a reasonable sweep. It embraces both the classical period of widening empire abroad and widening franchise at home, when Britain was said to be the mother of parliaments, and the more modern period when, perhaps since 1918, certainly since 1945, we have been endeavouring to find a new balance as a medium-sized power. For 43 of those 150 years Britain has been governed by overt coalitions, sometimes almost all-embracing as in 1915–16 and in the Churchill government of 1940–45, and sometimes more politically skewed, as with the Unionist coalition of 1895–1905, the Lloyd George coalition in its peacetime manifestation of 1919–22, and the National government of 1931–40, but all involving a wider or narrower degree of cross-party co-operation.

46.   In addition there have been 34 years in which the government of the day was dependent on the votes of another party (in one case of two others), although their representatives were not at the Cabinet table. Examples of this type of situation were provided by the Salisbury government of 1886-92, by the Asquith government between the first 1910 general election and the formation of the 1915 coalition, by the two short inter-war Labour governments and by parts of the Wilson/Callaghan government of 1974–79 when Liberal votes were crucial.

47.   And on top of these two periods of 43 and 34 years respectively there has to be added another nine years in which the government of the day, while technically in possession of an overall majority, had it by such an exiguous margin as to give no certain command over the arbitrament of the division lobby. This was the case in the last year and a half of the Attlee government, the first year and a half of the 1964 Wilson government and during much of John Major's experience with the Parliament of 1992–97. It is therefore the case that in only 64 of the past 150 years has there prevailed the alleged principal benefit of the FPTP system, the production of a single-party government with an undisputed command over the House of Commons.

48. On the factual record it clearly cannot be sustained that (*pace* Disraeli) there is anything shockingly unfamiliar to the British tradition about governments depending upon a broader basis than single party whipped votes in the House of Commons. Nor could it be plausibly argued, as is sometimes theoretically maintained, that such a wider basis carries with it such a burden of compromise as to produce inspissated immobility in decision making. Some of the most formative (for good or ill) of the changes of the period under review have occurred during coalition or minority governments, or as a result of a crucial cross-party vote, even when the government itself had a nominal one-party majority. These include: (i) the mid-nineteenth century reform of the fiscal system which turned Britain from a country of sinecures and protected privileges into the foremost market economy and free trade country of the world; (ii) the imposition from 1886 (with a gap from 1892-5), as an alternative to Home Rule, of 'twenty years of resolute government' upon Ireland, (iii) the Parliament Act of 1911 with the major shift towards the elective sovereignty of the House of Commons which that implied; (iv) the National Insurance Act of 1912 and hence the beginning of the welfare state; (v) victory, whatever the price, in the First World War; (vi) the move from free trade to imperial preference in the early 1930s; (vii) the survival of the country and hence of Western civilisation in the early 1940s, and (viii) the entry into Europe in the early 1970s.

49. History within a British context does not therefore suggest that single-party government, while it undoubtedly has strong virtues, as will be expounded below, is a necessary pre-requisite for effective action. Coalitions are by no means necessarily flaccid or indecisive. Nor is this view contradicted by geographical comparisons. Two of our near neighbours operate under one or other of the two main branches of proportional systems, and while recognising that what works well in one country does not necessarily do so in another, it is nonetheless worthwhile to consider briefly their respective experiences

The Republic of Ireland

50. The Republic of Ireland has operated under a Single Transferable Vote electoral system since the first days of the Irish Free State in 1922. This was fostered by the British in the last days of London rule mainly as a form of protection for the Protestant minority, but was in no way resisted by the new Irish government. (It was also introduced in Northern Ireland when Stormont was set up, but was then abolished by the Ulster Unionists in 1928 with the clear objective of strengthening one-party control in a two-community province.) In the Republic it has persisted, despite being twice put to a referendum by governments of Fianna Fáil, the party which thought it had most to gain from a majoritarian system. The proposal for a change was defeated on both occasions. The first was in 1959 when it went down by 52% to 48%; this vote however coincided with a presidential election when Eamon de Valera, the candidate of the party proposing the change was overwhelmingly elected. On the second occasion, in 1968, the proposition to move away from the Single Transferable Vote was more clearly rejected by 61% to 39%.

51. The Irish multi-member constituencies have been rather small – three to five members – for achieving the full proportional potential of the Single Transferable Vote. For this seven to eight member constituencies are better. As a result the Irish results have sometimes been little more than halfway between what FPTP would have produced and full proportionality. But

they have never failed to be well nearer to a fair representation of the competing parties than would have been the results under FPTP. Nor have they led to any divorce between TDs (Irish MPs) and localities. This has perhaps been made easier by the fact that Ireland is a small country. But, if anything, the complaint has been the reverse, that TDs are too locally and not enough nationally orientated. Members of the same party are often fighting as much or more against each other (in the constituencies) as they are against their opponents.

52. What have been the consequences for the political tone and the general performance of Ireland? The system has frequently but far from invariably produced coalition governments. Fianna Fáil was in independent power for two continuous periods each of sixteen years, from 1932 to 1948 and from 1957 to 1973. There have been occasional periods of instability, but scarcely more so than there have been in Britain (1922–24, 1950–1, 1974) under the FPTP system. Coalitions have become more frequent over the past twenty years or so, and there has also been some proliferation of parties (beyond the previous 2½ party pattern – Fianna Fáil, Fine Gael and Labour) over the same period. But this is little more than in line with the erosion of the two-party duopoly which has occurred in Britain over the same span. On the whole there has been no excessive frequency either of elections or of changes of government. Indeed, particularly in the long de Valera years, the greater charge against the Irish system was that it produced a dead hand of immobilism.

53. More recently there have been continuous coalitions (with the Irish Labour party co-operating at different times with both Fianna Fáil and Fine Gael), and perhaps a certain anonymity of leadership. Since de Valera there have been only a few Taoiseachs whose personality has lastingly impressed itself on the outside public. But this anonymity has by no means necessarily reflected itself in bad government. If the object of government is not to make a show for an international audience but to improve the lot of the governed, Ireland has done spectacularly well. From Cosgrave to Lynch to Fitzgerald to Haughey to Bruton to Reynolds to Ahern there has been stability on the most important aspect of policy, which has been that of co-operating fully with the European Community or Union so as to get the maximum benefit, both psychological (releasing Dublin from enmity as well as from subservience to London) and material, but using the substantial material aid not as a dole but as a springboard. The result has been a spectacular economic performance, with Irish national income per head now the rough equivalent of that of Britain, an equality which would have been simply inconceivable thirty years ago.

54. Furthermore, in the somewhat longer perspective of around eighty years, a polity born to an almost unexampled degree in destructive violence, first against the external 'oppressor' and then between different wings of the 'liberators', has settled down into a cosy and prosperous bourgeois society, the spirit of which is well expressed by the present day self-confident urbanity of Dublin. It would not be remotely sensible to argue that this has all been due to the benefit of the Single Transferable Vote. Equally, however, it is a piece of significant evidence that a more proportional system accompanied by coalition governments is in no way incompatible with a great advance in a country's performance.

Germany

55.   Some would dismiss Ireland as a small country: what works for 3½ million is very different from what might do so in a Britain of 58½ million. This consideration cannot apply to Germany, a country of 81½ million (or, perhaps more relevantly, of 65½ million, for the record essentially depends upon the performance of West Germany between 1949 and 1991), where with occasional small modifications a different form of proportional representation, the Additional Member System, has prevailed since the setting up of the Federal Republic. The additional members amount to the high proportion of 50% of the Bundestag. This gives a very strong degree of proportionality, substantially more so than with the Irish fairly small multiple member constituencies system of the Single Transferable Vote. It also gives a very high degree of party control over who is elected on the supplementary lists, a problem which there arouses less controversy than it would do here.

56.   What, however, is more relevant to the present stage of the argument is the extent to which it makes coalitions inevitable, and the effect which this has had upon the stability and quality of German governments. The answer to the first point is that it has undoubtedly made coalition the norm, but not inevitable. Adenauer, who was four times elected Chancellor by the Bundestag following a general election, was necessarily a coalition Chancellor on two of these occasions, 1949 and 1961. After the 1953 election he (together with the Bavarian CSU branch of his CDU party) had a bare absolute majority, and could have governed alone, but chose to continue the coalition with the Free Democrats over which he had presided since 1949. After the 1957 election he had a much bigger majority and dropped the FDP to form what was in effect a one-party government. (He still had the small Deutsche (or refugee) Partei in his government, but it had become as much his creature as the National or Simonite Liberals eventually did of the Conservatives in Britain). After 1961, which was a setback election for him, Adenauer was again dependent upon the FDP, and his remaining two years were not a success, but that was because he was over 85 and nearly everyone thought that it was time that he went.

57.   Before this overstay of welcome set in, however, the achievements of Adenauer were awe-inspiring. He began with a Germany that was shattered, impoverished and reviled, and he ended with one which was rich, respected and even admired. Its real national income had grown threefold under his Chancellorship, it had regained such sovereignty as was possible in an inter-dependent world, had become America's dependable and valued ally as well as the economic powerhouse of the Common Market, had buried a hundred years of Franco-German enmity and begun a Bonn-Paris partnership which was to run the European Community for at least a third of a century. And this massive constructive work was achieved just as much when he was in coalition as when he was nominally untrammelled.

58.   Since the end of Adenauer, coalition has been the unbroken pattern in Germany, though it has not always taken the same form. Mostly the FDP has been the hinge, and has done very well out of the rôle. But this was not so in 1966–69 when the two bigger parties formed a so-called 'Grand Coalition' and the FDP was excluded. From 1969 to 1982 that party was in alliance with the Social Democrats, and the centre-left, first under Brandt and then under Schmidt, was in continuous power.

59.   Then the FDP made a 'historic shift' and thirteen years of Brandt/Schmidt were succeeded by sixteen years of Kohl. It can certainly be argued, as we do at paragraph 122, that the German system has given too much power to the FDP. But it was not just a whim of this third party which was at work in 1982. In the election which followed in 1983 the CDU/CSU polled 48.8% as against their 44.9% of 1972 and the SDP fell from 45.8 to 38.2%. The FDP switch was working with the grain rather than against it. It was also a time of movement to the right in America and Britain. The FDP could more easily be accused of jumping on a band-wagon more than of perversely frustrating the desires of the electorate. Furthermore, the 1982 reversal of alliances apart, they never acted in a way that had not been made clear to the voters before an election.

60.   As this potted history makes clear, the last fault which could be attributed to proportional representation in Germany is that of instability of government. Over the 49 years which passed between the inauguration of the Federal Republic in 1949 and the 1998 election there were only six Chancellors. All of them, with the possible exception of Kurt-Georg Kiesinger, who presided over the Grand Coalition, were powerful world statesmen in their different ways. And no government or parliament has lasted less than three years. In Britain, on the other hand there have been no fewer than eleven Prime Ministers during the same period and three parliaments which have not survived for even two years. And even in the United States, with its fixed-term rigidities, there have been ten Presidents.

61.   If there has been a criticism of the recent working of the German system it is that it has produced too much rather than too little stability, that it has been sclerotic rather than febrile. In September 1998, however, a full-scale change of government occurred as a direct result of an election. Confidence was withdrawn from the previous government just as decisively as it was from the previous British government in 1997, although of course without the swollen majority which is a feature of FPTP. But a more significant point is that the system has produced not only stable but also, on the whole and judged by results, very good government. At least until the last seven years, when the awkward and ill-prepared dish of East Germany has proved difficult to digest even by the great boa-constrictor of the West German economy, the past half-century record of the Federal Republic has been remarkable. Judged by almost any available standard: economic success, a liberal and tolerant régime at home, an unassertive but responsible foreign policy, it is difficult to find any major country which, over the past half century, has been better or indeed as well governed. In any event this would be a great achievement. In view of Germany's previous recent history, it is almost a miracle. Once again it would be ludicrous to attribute all this to the Additional Member System of proportional representation. But it is at least strong evidence that such a system, and the coalition habit in which, with a 50:50 constituency/top-up member balance, it mostly results, is not necessarily an inhibition on such a favourable outcome.

Other Countries

62.   There are of course other foreign comparisons which are commonly regarded as much less favourable to the case for proportional systems. Those most frequently cited are Israel, Italy, the France of the Fourth Republic (1946–58) and (latterly and perhaps most prominently) New Zealand. They each raise somewhat separate issues. Israel operates on a

national list system with a very low threshold, so that small splinter parties easily get representation in the Knesset and can sometimes be decisive to the formation or support of a government. It can be stated straightaway that, from the beginning of its deliberations the Commission has rejected such a national list system for Britain. It would, in our view, be too remote, rigid and party machine-dominated a system for our four-nation and regionally diverse polity of 58½ million people. It would also run directly counter to our fourth requirement, that of a link between MPs and a geographical constituency. It should nonetheless be noted in passing that a national list system works on the whole well in the Netherlands, a country of 15½ million (as opposed to Israel's 5½ million). Its disadvantage there, as some would see it, is that it makes all governments coalitions and that after elections these mostly take some time to negotiate. But, once negotiated, and the negotiations are open rather than 'smoke-filled', they have considerable stability and nearly always last a full parliament. Furthermore it would be difficult to contest the view that the Netherlands is one of the most successfully governed countries in the world, combining a growth economy, a non-inflationary currency and a society more at ease with itself than most in the Western world.

Italy

63.   Italy is frequently held up as the *locus classicus* of the evils of a proportional system. It is certainly true that it practised a list system with a threshold of 2% on the basis of large regions for nearly fifty years from the establishment of the republic in 1946, and that this coincided with bewilderingly frequent changes of government. There were 29 switches of Prime Minister during this period, although the cast was revolving as well as large: 18 individuals headed the 29 governments. Paradoxically, there was also a considerable, arguably too much, stability of policy. The Christian Democrats, at least as broad as the Church of England, were always the core of every government, with a fringe of various coalition partners. The instability was essentially that of political personnel, which had the effect of rendering the political class somewhat irrelevant. The non-elected administrators, filling a vacuum, perhaps achieved more power than is healthy in a democracy. This was particularly true of the Banca d'Italia and of the Italian Foreign Ministry, both of which performed with distinction and consistency. Despite the frequent changes at the top there was a good deal more steadiness of Italian economic and foreign policy in, say, the twenty-five years from 1955 to 1980 than there was of British policy in these fields. And this showed itself both in a more successful Italian than British handling of relations with the European Community and of a much stronger Italian rate of economic growth. It is clear, however, that the Italians were concerned about the rapid turnover of governments, and attributed this at least in part the electoral system. As a result, they changed in 1993 to a variant of the German Additional Member System, not, as has been erroneously reported, to FPTP.

64.   Underneath the electoral system, however, there were two deep fractures in Italian society. The first was that over a century after the exploits of Garibaldi's 'Thousand' the old Kingdom of the Two Sicilies, with its weak civic culture, remains fundamentally unintegrated into the successful Italy of the north and the centre. The second was that the Communist Party of Italy, while always more open, moderate and penetrating of bourgeois life (films and publishing for example) than was the French Communist party, nonetheless occupied for

decades the awkward position of being sufficiently strong to block the emergence of any other mass opposition to the ruling Christian Democrats, while sufficiently 'way out' to make any government with Communist participation unacceptable to the Catholic Church, to the United States (always a crucial factor in post-war Italy) and maybe to the leaders of the European Community. As a result there could be no easy and natural alternation of governments in Italy, and with this major safety valve unavailable, a superficial instability provided a minor and unsatisfactory alternative. These two fractures have been a much more fundamental cause of Italian political weakness than has been its electoral system. That 1946–93 system was not however one which this Commission would contemplate recommending for Britain. Since then, the knot at the heart of Italian politics has been loosened by the old PCI (Communist Party of Italy, not to be confused with the rump Refundazione Communista) changing both its name and its policies, moving further into the mainstream, and becoming part of the 'Olive coalition' with which Romano Prodi has successfully governed for 2½ years until this autumn. The rump party has however retained enough power to be the catalyst for defeating the Prodi Government by one vote earlier this month. Such a narrow defeat can, however, happen under almost any political and electoral system. It was exactly the fate which in 1979 met James Callaghan after only a few months longer in office.

France

65.   On France the British Conservative party's powerful memorandum of evidence to us stated that "it is well-known that PR contributed to the instability of governments in the French Fourth Republic (which is why it was repealed in 1958)". Once again it is undeniable that the Fourth Republican list system did coincide with frequent changes of government – there were twenty in the twelve years between de Gaulle's two periods of power. And there was also, with the exception of Mendès-France's effective nine months in 1954–55, a persistent weakness of government. Nevertheless there were some significant achievements: the launch of the Schuman Plan, the modernisation of the French economy under the Commissariat du Plan, which laid the foundation for much of the economic success of the Fifth Republic, and the difficult but necessary withdrawal from Indo-China. The peculiar difficulty that the French had in winding down their colonial empire – with Algeria even more traumatic than Indo-China – was a continuing cause of weakness and instability. This, and the fact that each National Assembly for its five years of life was effectively immune from either the threat of dissolution or the responsibility, when it had defeated one government, for finding another (in sharp contrast with the duty laid upon the German Bundestag of not being able to vote out one government without providing another) had at least as much to do with the deficiencies of the régime as did the electoral system.

66.   Furthermore, the experience of France in the lead up to the 1940 collapse makes it very difficult to lay the blame for national weakness at the door of a proportional electoral system. Between 1919 and 1927 France had got along under a proportional multi-member system known as *scrutin de liste*. Then it was changed for the last twelve years of that Republic to *scrutin d'arrondissement*, which was very similar to the British system with single member constituencies and simple pluralities, although with two ballots as in the France of today. As those twelve years terminated in the collapse of 1940 it could be argued that the agent of

disaster was the switch to a single member majoritarian system. But it would be much wiser not to, and to recognise that there are factors more fundamental and more complicated than its electoral system in the strength or weakness of a nation and its régime, and that what can work well in certain countries and circumstances can work badly in others, and *vice-versa*. Fractured societies are more powerful than voting systems, good or bad, in producing failures of government.

New Zealand

67.   The fourth overseas comparison which has recently come to be cited adversely to the case for electoral reform is that of New Zealand. New Zealand, which had previously used, with small modification, the FPTP system as currently practised in Britain, moved after the 1993 general election and a referendum to what is there called Mixed Member Proportional (MMP) and is very close to the German system with both countries using FPTP for constituency elections and a near-equal balance between constituency and list seats. The general election of 1996 is so far the only one in New Zealand to have been fought under the new rules. There have been wide reports of early disenchantment with the new system, which the Commission took sufficiently seriously to think it wise to send a delegation of three of its members to investigate. Their clear report was that while dissatisfaction might well lead to a further referendum (there was always provision for an early review) and some modification of the MMP system, it was the nearly unanimous opinion of politicians and other opinion makers that there was unlikely to be a simple reversion to FPTP. Such nearly unanimous punditry can of course be wrong. But there are nonetheless some substantial reasons for thinking that it may be modification of the new system rather than reversion to the old which the New Zealand electorate will favour. There are also some considerable lessons of relevance here to be drawn from striking a balance sheet of the pros and cons of the brief New Zealand experience.

68.   Apparently on the adverse side of the balance sheet is the behaviour of the New Zealand First party. There is, however, at least an even chance that it would have held a hinge position even had the election been fought under the previous FPTP system. It was a new party, although containing a few old politicians, which in the 1996 general election campaigned vigorously against the National party government of Mr Bolger. And it was a substantial beneficiary of that campaign. It secured 17 seats (or 14.2% of the total), eleven of them by list rather than by direct election. This gave it a key position, with Labour on 37 seats, the National party on 44, the Alliance party on 13 and others on 9. It was not however much beyond their deserts, for they had secured 13½% of the votes. After an eight week interregnum New Zealand First then proceeded to form a coalition, not as had been expected with the Labour party, but with the National party, which they had so freely denounced during the campaign. Neither the delay not the apparent reversal of alliance created a good impression. Nor was it markedly beneficial to the fickle party. New Zealand First secured 5 (out of 20) Cabinet posts, but its poll rating fell quickly from 14% to 1%. The party has since split and partially withdrawn from the coalition.

69.   There have been two other aspects of the new system which have militated against its popularity. The first was that it was associated with an increase in the size of the Parliament from 99 to 120 members. (This in relation to size of electorate would be equivalent to increasing a British House of Commons with already 1794 members to one of 2175.) It was not popular, for a lack of respect for existing MPs was a considerable factor in producing the referendum vote for a change. The electorate did not want more of them. The British House of Commons with a membership of 659 is today one of the biggest legislative assemblies in the world. Many think it would function better if smaller. That is well outside our terms of reference. But one conclusion we draw from the New Zealand experience is that we should avoid any solution which involves even a small increase in the size of the House of Commons.

70.   The other factor which seems to have disappointed the New Zealand electorate has been the failure of the new system to produce any reduction in the rancour and bitterness of party politics. There was apparently a widespread desire and hope that MMP would lead to a more consensual political habit. This had been a marked feature of its near twin AMS in Germany. In the Federal Republic, with its elaborate system of power-sharing between Länder and not very centralised central government, and within the federal legislature between Bundestag and Bundesrat (the latter made up of Länder representatives, often with different parties in power in the different institutions), a consensual habit has become the dominant political culture.

71.   New Zealand, on the other hand, with its unicameral legislature and weak local government, was unusually free of any such checks and balances. The public hope that the new system would lead to politicians taking more notice of their opponents has however been sadly disappointed. The 'shot-gun marriage' between National and New Zealand First, while producing only a parliamentary majority of one, nevertheless proceeded to govern with considerable intransigence. It seized the Speakership, the deputy Speakership and 15 out of 17 committee chairmanships, while also forcing through after minimal discussion a highly controversial budget and finance bill as well as other far from consensual legislation.

72.   Considerable off-setting factors are however widely perceived in New Zealand. The first is that the current parliament is seen as being the most representative which has ever there been elected. The proportion of women members has risen to 30%, the Maoris have for the first time achieved a representation approximately equal to their numerical strength, and there is also a hitherto unknown presence of Asian and South Sea Islander MPs. Few in New Zealand would want to lose this better balance.

73.   It is also the case that the New Zealand electorate seem to appreciate the greater degree of voter choice offered by the new system. In 1996 37% of those voting – a much higher proportion than in Germany – chose to split the party affiliation of their two votes, thereby liberating their choice of local members from their view of what party or combination should form the government of the country. Nor did they show any evidence of finding the new system confusing. 87% of them turned out to vote and cast valid ballots. For these reasons amongst others, while it is impossible to pretend that the country's early experience of MMP has been fortunate, it is unlikely that it will opt to go back to FPTP as opposed to some modification of the new system.

Australia

74.   The next international comparison we make is perhaps the one with most resonance for the United Kingdom. Australia is often referred to as the most governed country in the world with three distinct, but interrelated layers of Government at local, regional and national or federal level. It is the latter in which we have most interest. At national level Australia is governed by a bicameral parliament with direct elections to both Houses. Members of the House of Representatives (the lower house) are elected using the Alternative Vote, or the Single Transferable Vote in single member constituencies as it sometimes called there, while members of the Senate (the upper house) are elected on a more proportional basis using the Single Transferable Vote in multi-member constituencies. Compulsory voting ensures that turn-out at elections is very high, generally exceeding 95%.

75.   The relationship between the two Houses and their respective electoral systems is key to understanding Australia's polity. The systems operate in tandem to deliver stable government with constituency members elected on a majority vote and normally delivering 'single'-party majority Government in the House of Representatives (in Australia the National Party and Liberal Party are in almost indissoluble alliance which means that the Commonwealth is effectively a two-party society). Wider representation or proportionality is delivered through the Senate. Unlike the House of Lords *vis-à-vis* the House of Commons the Senate has broadly the same powers as the House of Representatives. This and the fact that it is rare for the Government to hold a majority in both Houses makes it a powerful check on the executive. The Australian electorate and politicians appear at ease with their electoral systems, which have on the whole worked effectively since 1919. In the October 1998 election Pauline Hanson's much apprehended extreme One Nation Party failed as a result of the Alternative Vote even to retain the seat of its leader, and the Liberal/National Alliance was returned to power with a working majority in the lower house, but as it had substantially fewer votes than the Labour Party, this was a still more perverse result than the British ones of 1951 or 1974.

FPTP Shared Mainly with North America and India

76.   It is difficult to find in the post-1945 years examples beyond India, which is admittedly a big exception, although not one exhibiting great stability since the prestige of the Nehru/Gandhi Congress party faded, of a country making an unfettered choice, as opposed to accepting an inheritance, in favour of FPTP. None of the new democracies of the first decade of freedom in central and eastern Europe appear to have contemplated going in that direction. If there is a trend, it is towards incorporating a degree of constituency representation, and in some cases moving away from pure proportionality (while retaining a significant proportional corrective mechanism).

77.   FPTP we share with the United States and with Canada. The United States is of course the most powerful democracy in the world, with an impressive record of world leadership for nearly the past sixty years. On the other hand it is a presidential and not a parliamentary system in the British sense (which may be good or bad but weakens the comparison), its level of participation in elections, at barely 50% for Presidential elections and only 37% in the last mid-term Congressional elections, is appallingly low, and some would say that its system of

government has not recently been a great advertisement for democratic maturity. The Canadian political record was for long an impressive one, but it has not recently produced much stability (the previously governing Conservative party was reduced to two seats at the 1989 election) or successful national unity. While it would be wrong to attribute the Quebec problem to FPTP, it would also be wrong to say that Canadian experience provides evidence for FPTP being a nationally unifying system.

Chapter Five: Solutions for Britain Without Constituency Changes

78.   It is time to turn to the specifically British aspects of the issue. The problem here has obviously become more acute since the electoral watershed of the post-war period in 1974. Prior to the first of the two elections of that year British politics was overwhelmingly a two-party affair and although FPTP did not work perfectly (as in the perverse 1951 result, and in the bottling up of sporadic third party surges, which were only allowed to show themselves in by-elections) it did not represent a major and manifest unfairness between parties. Since that date approximately 20% of the voting public (26% in 1983) have turned away from the two-horse race(see Table 1 below). In these circumstances those who resist change have to argue that the preference of a fifth to a quarter of the nation is irresponsibly inimical to the British tradition, and that such a considerable proportion ought either to be forced back into a more acceptable pattern of behaviour or effectively ignored.

Table 1

Year	Conservatives		Labour		Liberals/ Lib Dems		Nationalist parties	
	% vote	% seats	% vote	% seats	% vote	% seats	% vote	% seats
1945	39.8	33.3	48.3	61.4	9.1	1.9	0.2	—
1950	43.5	47.7	46.1	50.4	9.1	1.4	0.1	—
1951	48.0	51.4	48.8	47.2	2.5	1.0	0.1	—
1955	49.7	54.6	46.4	44.0	2.7	1.0	0.2	—
1959	49.4	57.9	43.8	41.0	5.9	1.0	0.4	—
1964	43.4	48.3	44.1	50.3	11.2	1.4	0.5	—
1966	41.9	40.2	47.9	57.6	8.5	1.9	0.7	—
1970	46.4	52.4	43.0	45.6	7.5	1.0	1.3	0.2
Feb'74	37.9	46.8	37.1	47.4	19.3	2.2	2.6	1.4
Oct'74	35.8	43.6	39.2	50.2	18.3	2.1	3.5	2.2
1979	43.9	53.4	36.9	42.4	13.8	1.7	2.0	0.6
1983	42.4	61.0	27.6	32.0	25.4	3.5	1.5	0.6
1987	42.3	57.8	30.9	35.2	22.6	3.4	1.7	0.9
1992	41.9	51.6	34.3	41.6	17.9	3.1	2.3	1.0
1997	30.7	25.0	43.2	63.6	16.8	7.0	2.5	1.5

79.   This is not an unarguable proposition. Indeed it can be and is argued, often with considerable force and some persuasiveness. But it requires as essential premises the views both that FPTP has served us peculiarly well, and that a deviation from it would be demonstrably deleterious. So far as the first is concerned it is undoubtedly true that Britain has long enjoyed an unusually stable parliamentary régime (broadening into a democracy between 1832 and 1918, or 1969 if age as well as class and sex enfranchisement are taken into account) and that this has on the whole been accompanied by a tolerant, decent and sometimes successful society. It is however much more difficult to argue that these qualities have been directly linked to the exact electoral system, and would have been gravely endangered if the

recommendations of the 1917 Speaker's Conference for a mixture of the Single Transferable Vote in the big towns and cities and the Alternative Vote in the rest of the country, or the 1930 House of Commons endorsement of the Alternative Vote (rejected by the Lords) had been implemented. And if the criterion be economic success it would be still more difficult to argue that the British performance, particularly over the past 40 years, gives a clear endorsement to FPTP. Nor does the respect in which Parliament is currently held, or the turn-out at elections, or the degree of commitment to the political process exhibited, particularly by the young, constitute a ringing endorsement of the present system.

80.   Against this background we have approached the question of what alternative system we should recommend for Britain. We do so by no means rejecting the achievements of the British political tradition, but being anxious to build upon and improve it, such flexible improvement being indeed very much part of the tradition. We do so also after observing the virtues and deficiencies of different systems abroad, without believing that any is perfect, but finding that there is nonetheless a lot to learn from objective comparative appraisal.

The Alternative Vote

81.   The simplest change would be from FPTP to the Alternative Vote (henceforth referred to as AV). This meets several of our four criteria. It would fully maintain the link between MPs and a single geographical constituency. It would increase voter choice in the sense that it would enable voters to express their second and sometimes third or fourth preferences, and thus free them from a bifurcating choice between realistic and ideological commitment or, as it sometimes is called, voting tactically. There is not the slightest reason to think that AV would reduce the stability of government; it might indeed lead to larger parliamentary majorities. This is a formidable list of assets, particularly in the context of our terms of reference. And there are at least two further ones. AV would involve no change of constituency boundaries, and could thus be implemented from the moment that Parliament accepted a positive vote in a referendum. It would also virtually ensure that each MP commanded at least majority acquiescence within his constituency, which is far from being the case under FPTP, where as we have seen nearly a half of members have more opponents than supporters, and, exceptionally, a member can be elected (as in Inverness in 1992) with as little as 26% of the vote. However, it is necessary to acknowledge the argument that the second or subsequent preferences of a losing candidate, if they are decisive, are seen by some as carrying less value (and even as arising almost accidentally) and so contributing less to the legitimacy of the result, than first preference votes (or indeed the second preferences of the most powerful candidates).

82.   Beyond this AV on its own suffers from a stark objection. It offers little prospect of a move towards greater proportionality, and in some circumstances, and those the ones which certainly prevailed at the last election and may well do so for at least the next one, it is even less proportional that FPTP. Simulations of how the 1997 result might have come out under AV suggest that it would have significantly increased the size of the already swollen Labour majority. A 'best guess' projection of the shape of the current Parliament under AV suggests on one highly reputable estimate the following outcome with the actual FPTP figures given in brackets after the projected figures: Labour 452 (419), Conservative 96 (165), Liberal Democrats 82 (46), others 29 (29). The overall Labour majority could thus have risen from 169

to 245. On another equally reputable estimate the figures are given as Labour 436, Conservatives 110, Liberal Democrats 84 and others 29, an overall majority this time of 213. On either basis an injustice to the Liberal Democrats would have been nearly two-thirds corrected (their strictly proportional entitlement was 111 seats) but at the price of a still greater injustice to the Conservatives. The Conservative 30.7% of the votes should strictly have given them 202 seats. Instead FPTP gave them 165 or 25% of the seats, whereas AV would have given them on one estimate only 96 (or 14.6% of the seats), and on the more favourable one from their point of view 110 seats (or 16.7% of the total).

83.   The 1997 election, it can be argued, was far from typical. The scenario was the one most calculated to produce an exaggerated majority and to increase disproportionality. There was a strong desire to get rid of the incumbent government, the third party (Liberal Democrats) was much closer to the main Labour challenger than to the government, and many voters cared more about casting an anti-Conservative vote than about whether this would result in a Labour or a Liberal Democrat victory in their particular constituency. (This last factor, however, did not clearly add to the difference between a FPTP and an AV result, for many electors did a sort of 'do it yourself' AV and voted for whichever of the two opposition candidates they thought was the more effective challenger.) In the three previous elections, those of 1983, 1987 and 1992, AV would have had a less distorting effect on proportionality between the two main parties. For example, one estimate suggests that it would have led to a Conservative majority (with the actual FPTP result again given in brackets) of 27 (21) in 1992. But it would have avoided this distortion at the expense of being able to claim much less credit for correcting the adverse treatment of the third party. The Liberal Democrats would in 1992 have got only 31 or 4.8% of the seats for 19% of the vote.

84.   Added to this, AV on its own, because it makes use exclusively of single-member constituencies, would fail to address several of the more significant defects of FPTP which we identified earlier. In particular, there would still be large tracts of the country which would be electoral deserts for major parties. Conservative voters in Scotland, for example, might only hope to influence the result through their second choice. And although AV would probably increase the number of marginal seats thus reducing the number of voters effectively excluded from influencing the overall result, most seats in the country would remain safe.

85.   The Commission's conclusions from these and other pieces of evidence about the operation of AV are threefold. First, it does not address one of our most important terms of reference. So far from doing much to relieve disproportionality, it is capable of substantially adding to it. Second, its effects (on its own without any corrective mechanism) are disturbingly unpredictable. Third, it would in the circumstances of the last election, which even if untypical is necessarily the one most vivid in the recollection of the public, and very likely in the circumstances of the next one too, be unacceptably unfair to the Conservatives. Fairness in representation is a complex concept, as we have seen in paragraph 6, and one to which the upholders of FPTP do not appear to attach great importance. But it is one which, apart from anything else, inhibits a Commission appointed by a Labour government and presided over by a Liberal Democrat from recommending a solution which at the last election might have left

the Conservatives with less than half of their proportional entitlement. We therefore reject the AV as *on its own* a solution despite what many see as its very considerable advantage of ensuring that every constituency member gains majority acquiescence.

The Supplementary Vote

86.   With it there falls in our view, the Supplementary Vote or SV. It is a system close to AV, and is likely to produce a very similar result. As such it shares many of the disadvantages of AV and some of the advantages, although not the major one of making each MP, at the last count, a majority choice. Its essential difference from AV is that it allows the voter to exercise only a second choice, and not a third, a fourth or even a fifth one, and thus avoids these weak, even haphazard lower-grade choices, as some would argue, from occasionally illegitimately influencing the result. It is much more suited to a three rather than a four party political scenario, and would therefore cause special difficulties in Scotland and Wales. Essentially, however, the deficiencies which we regard as endemic to AV apply almost equally to SV. If they could be overcome, the choice, in England at any rate, between AV or SV would be a finely balanced one.

The Second Ballot System

87.   A cousin of SV is the French system of two ballots or *deuxième tour*. This cannot be wholly convincingly dismissed by Labour and Conservatives opposed to any change in the electoral system for it is near to the method they have both recently used for the choice of their party leader, and therefore in many cases of an actual or future Prime Minister. These elections were in consequence peculiarly important, carrying a choice of far more moment for the limited parliamentary electorate than does a choice of local MP for the run of constituency voters. Yet neither Conservatives nor Labour have in any contested election this century thought of entrusting this grave decision to the vagaries of a FPTP system. Of course in an election for a single position, whether it be leader of a party, President of a Republic, or Mayor of London, the more complicated but at least arguably fairer systems, such as the Single Transferable Vote or the Additional Member System, are by definition inapplicable. If only one is to be elected it is not possible to achieve a balance. A true majoritarian decision is the best for which it is then possible to go.

88.   Nevertheless, despite its place in British party history, the second ballot is not a solution which the Commission is disposed to recommend. It suffers from nearly all the deficiencies of AV. In addition, like SV, it does not guarantee that each MP has majority support or at least acquiescence. It would involve the British electorate going twice to the polls, with many of them showing a considerable reluctance to go even once. And it necessarily involves a poll being spread over a minimum of one week. Until 1918 British general elections were spread over a longer period than is the current French habit but because of staggered polling days in different constituencies and not because of a second ballot. Despite this precedent such a spread would be inimical to the quick, sharp change of government (when that is the verdict of the electorate) which has become the British practice since 1945.

The 'Weighted' Vote

89.   It should however perhaps be mentioned in passing that there is another system operating entirely on existing constituencies, apart from those systems which have already been discussed and rejected, which has been advocated by a number of those providing us with written submissions. It is what might be called the "weighted vote member system". Members would be elected exactly as now, but where their party was under-represented nationally this would be corrected by giving them an additional voting strength in the division lobbies of the House of Commons. Thus, to take an extreme example, a Liberal Democrat (then Alliance) member in the 1983 Parliament would have been entitled to cast 7½ votes in any division, and more typically, in the present Parliament a Conservative member would be entitled to 1¼ votes. Whether they would carry these numbers round their necks or on their backs, rather like prize bulls at an agricultural show, is not clear, but what is clear is that there would be great problems if one of these vote-heavy beasts were to find himself in a lobby different from his party leader and whips, or worse still, if he were permanently to lumber off across the floor. There would inevitably be the most excited attempts to re-corral him. And the ability sometimes to take independent action must surely be preserved, even encouraged, if MPs are not to become party automata.

90.   Therefore, while we respect the ingenuity and conviction with which this weighted vote solution has been put forward, we think that it would arouse more mockery than enthusiasm and be incompatible with the practical working of a parliament.

Inevitable Consequence

91.   The Commission therefore believes that it can only discharge its duty of providing the electorate with a valid alternative choice to FPTP and come nearest to meeting its four criteria by accepting some modification of the one constituency/one member pattern. Otherwise it could make no contribution to fulfilling requirement (i), that of 'broad proportionality' and not enough to requirement (iii), that for 'an extension of voter choice'. However in view of requirement (iv), 'the maintenance of a link between MPs and geographical constituencies', it will endeavour to make this modification as limited as is reasonably effective.

Chapter Six: The Single Transferable Vote

92.   We therefore come to the two main families of reformed and more proportional systems, of which the first is the Single Transferable Vote (henceforth STV) in multi-member constituencies. It is a system which has several substantial advantages. It maximises voter choice, giving the elector power to express preference not only between parties but between different candidates of the same party. It achieves a significantly greater degree of proportionality. It avoids the problem of having two classes of member, as is the case with the Additional Member System. It also avoids the likelihood of fostering a proliferation of small splinter parties, and does this without the need for setting any arbitrary threshold. It has long worked with on the whole beneficial results in the Republic of Ireland (as we have seen), a country which had previously shared at least a part of the British parliamentary tradition. It has also just produced a clear cut change of government in Malta. And STV is in addition the system which commands the enthusiastic support of most of those who have devoted their minds and their energies to the cause of electoral reform.

93.   The Commission has therefore given it the most serious consideration. Out of this consideration it has become aware of a number of counterbalancing disadvantages, none of them individually decisive but which are fairly formidable in combination and even more so because they lead in to what in our view is the fatal objection to our currently recommending STV for Britain.

94.   In Britain, with a population of 58½ million as against Ireland's 3½ million, the constituencies (unless there were to be a massive increase in the number of MPs, which the Commission regards as unacceptable; see paragraph 69) would need to be approximately four or five times as large as the Irish constituencies. This would make them geographically far-flung in rural or semi-rural areas, and, even in concentrated urban areas, constituencies of about 350,000 electors would entail a very long ballot paper and a degree of choice which might be deemed oppressive rather than liberating.

95.   Lest this point should be thought contradictory to one of the favourable points listed above, and indeed given as one of the desiderata in our terms of reference, it should be stated that the Commission sees the extension of voter choice as highly desirable up to the point at which the average voter is able and eager meaningfully to exercise choice, both between and within parties. But that where the choice offered resembles a caricature of an over-zealous American breakfast waiter going on posing an indefinite number of unwanted options, it becomes both an exasperation and an incitement to the giving of random answers. In voting rather than in breakfast terms exasperation may discourage going to the polls at all and randomness lead to the casting of perverse or at least meaningless votes. Some people want to be able to choose between candidates of the same party, but many are interested only in voting for parties, and would not appreciate being forced into choosing between candidates of the same party about each of whom they know little.

96.   It is however the counting rather than the casting of the votes which is excessively complicated under STV. The Irish seem to have no particular difficulty in filling in their ballot papers. They have a somewhat but not vastly higher proportion of spoilt papers than in Britain, and they have recently had a somewhat but not much lower turnout. This latter factor is worth noting in view of the Irish tradition of almost excessively high voting. The differential is not nearly strong enough to erect a theory that STV discourages voting, but it is sufficient to cast doubt on any theory that the greater voter choice of STV positively encourages participation in the democratic process.

97.   The counting is incontestably opaque, although this is of course different from saying that it is haphazard or unfair. It may be doubted whether many Irish voters could explain exactly how it is done, but there are even fewer who complain about its lack of transparency. It is also the case that different systems of counting can produce different results for the candidates who are not elected in the first two or three for each constituency, but there can be an element of this in all systems which seek to correct the crude clarity of FPTP. This complexity (and consequent slowness) of counting should not be elevated into a fatal bar to STV, but nor can it be counted as an advantage.

98.   Apart from its inherent complexity it is also the case that STV suffers from the accidental disadvantage that it is a different system from those which are to be used for the European elections, the Scottish Parliament, the Welsh Assembly and the London Assembly. This is however to some extent counter-balanced by the fact that it is a system which Northern Ireland has used for over twenty years for filling its three seats in the European Parliament and has just successfully used for its own new Assembly. The Commission does not take the view that it should automatically follow what is already in place. It has, for instance, already rejected as unsuitable for the Westminster Parliament the list system which is now in place for the European Parliament. There is nonetheless an obvious disadvantage to burdening large parts of the voting public with getting used to several new systems within a short time-scale. It is also an odd quirk of STV that it has never been tried in a country which has not within this century been subject to British rule. Some might regard this as a qualification rather than a demerit, but it has the consequence that the polities in which experience of it has been gained are all relatively small. This is obviously true of the Republic of Ireland, of Northern Ireland and of Malta. The nearest approach to an exception is Australia, where STV is used in a modified form for elections to the Senate, a more powerful second chamber than the House of Lords. But even here Australia's population of 16 million makes it barely a quarter the size of Britain.

99.   There was also a point critical of STV which was put to us by a number of leading Irish politicians – although with one or two voices the other way – whom we saw on our visit to Dublin, and which left us with the impression that STV in Ireland is perhaps more popular with the public than with the politicians. If this be so it is difficult to know whether to score the point in the favourable or in the adverse list. Many would think that the opinion of the sovereign people is much more important, and that if an electoral system is a shoe which pinches the politicians that is all to its credit. Nevertheless it is at least possible that the politicians may be better judges of what conduces to effective government.

100.   The point, for what it is worth, is that multi-member constituencies with MPs and candidates competing in them not merely against other parties but against members of their own party too, so far from producing remote representatives, produces excessively parochial ones. They are much keener on being in their constituencies pursuing local issues than they are on attending to their legislative and other national duties in the Dail. And, even when they are in Dublin, they are very loath to vote for a necessary but potentially unpopular measure until they know that their rival/partner from the same party in the same constituency is doing so too. There thus develops what may be described as an 'after you Cecil, after you Claud' mentality.

101.   It was also suggested that the constituent with a grievance does not so much go to the TD of his choice as go in turn to all three or four or five of them, according to the size of the constituency in which he or she lives, thereby wasting a good deal of the time of ministers, civil servants, TDs, and indeed of the constituents themselves. It could perhaps be said that, superimposed on an intensely local political culture, STV in Ireland has turned out to be a system more suited to the style of a good local councillor become a TD than to that of Daniel O'Connell or Charles Stewart Parnell. Nonetheless, of the two former Taoiseachs with whom we talked, one (although a firm upholder of some form of proportional system) agreed with this criticism, while the other was robustly of the view that good individual results under STV could be achieved and maintained just as much by national leadership as by intense local attention, and without any crippling constituency time commitment either.

STV as Part of a Hybrid Scheme

102.   Despite these disadvantages of varying orders of seriousness, the Commission regarded the force of the case for STV, arising out of a combination of its intellectual neatness, its unique practical contribution to voter choice, and its place in the hearts of the most dedicated electoral reformers, as sufficiently strong for very serious consideration to be given to whether it could not be found a place (and an opportunity to prove itself) in a hybrid scheme. Some members (particularly the chairman) were attracted by the recommendations of the 1917 Speaker's Conference. This provided, as we saw earlier, for STV in the large towns and cities accompanied by AV in the less urban and more scattered parts of the country.

103.   One argument in favour of such a hybrid approach is that it would enable the single member/single constituency link to be preserved in large parts of Britain (and those probably where it has most meaning) while adding an element of proportionality in the areas where it has less meaning (see paragraph 104). If conurbations down to the size of Bristol, Coventry and Cardiff together with some of the most concentrated urban areas of West Yorkshire and South Lancashire were chosen as STV areas it could give a proportionately elected core of approximately 250 MPs, and it could do so without any complicated re-drawing of constituency boundaries. The putting together of the existing Leeds or Liverpool constituencies with perhaps the addition of one or two clearly belonging satellite suburban ones, particularly bearing in mind that STV with its provision for minority representation is an inbuilt corrective to any attempt at a gerrymander, is much simpler – and less controversial – than the re-drawing of parliamentary boundaries within a city which is a fairly frequent feature of the present system.

104.   It is indeed this continual re-shuffling of big-city internal parliamentary boundaries which made the Commission feel that such a differential treatment might be an effective way of reconciling points (i) (broad proportionality) and (iv) (a geographical link between MPs and their constituencies). It may be accepted that there can be some sort of special and valuable link between a member and a broad-acred constituency on the one hand (say the Yorkshire Richmond or Huntingdon) or one with a concentrated and distinct community sense (say Blackburn or the old Ebbw Vale) on the other, without pretending that much mystical unity can be attached to the entity of Leicester South-East as opposed to that of Leicester South-West, particularly as the boundaries of 'points of the compass' constituencies (and it is little different where they have changing locality names as in Birmingham or Glasgow) are in a fairly constant state of flux. The example given to us at our public meeting in London of the voter who over an adult lifetime in the same house found himself in five different constituencies may be an unusual one, but it nonetheless illustrates, even if an extreme form, the truth that big-city constituencies are often more floating kidneys than natural communities, that MP identification is lower in them than in the country as a whole, and that, in the experience of the chairman of the Commission who has sat for the largest provincial city of England as well as for the largest city of any sort in Scotland, nearly a half of constituency duties relate to city-wide rather than to purely constituency-contained issues.

105.   There would thus be a certain rationale for treating the cities differently. Nevertheless the difficulty of explaining convincingly why nearly one half of the electorate were being asked to vote under a different system from the rest stands like a forbidding lion in the path of such a scheme. It would only be worth facing its fangs for a outcome which was manifestly beneficial from nearly every other point of view. And the Commission was ultimately unanimously persuaded that this would not be the case here. Just as it rejected AV as a solitary recipe on the ground that it would not be fair to those who support the Conservative party, so it rejected the hybrid system on the ground that, in addition to its complication, it would not, in most circumstances, be fair to those who support the Labour party. STV in the cities would let in minority Conservative representation to the Labour heartlands of the industrial centres of England, Scotland and Wales. That indeed would be part of the object of the exercise, and would in the view of the Commission be inherently desirable, for large tracts of one party monopoly are one of the major counts against FPTP. But a necessary corollary is that there should also be minority Labour representation in the areas where the Conservatives have long reigned supreme. This would be unlikely to be forthcoming. A Conservative MP for Liverpool would not be balanced by a Labour one for Surrey or Dorset.

106.   The fact that the Liberal Democrats would make substantial strides towards fairer treatment under both AV on its own and a mixture of AV and STV does not answer this point. It is desirable that there should be as much all-round equity as possible, and that involves the two major parties (somewhat complacently though they have long sat upon their privileged treatment under FPTP) just as much as it does the third party against which there has been heavy discrimination. On this ground, fortified by the need for a strong positive justification for a two-tier system, the Commission rejected, with some regret, the eighty-year old solution of the Speaker's Conference which would amongst its other real but insufficient advantages, have restored the parliamentary cohesion of the provincial metropolises.

Conclusion on STV Generally

107.   Apart from some inherent disadvantages – but no electoral system, including particularly FPTP, is a stranger to them – STV would be too big a leap from that to which we have become used, and it would be a leap in a confusingly different direction from the other electoral changes which are currently being made in Britain. It would also, particularly in the less densely populated areas of the country, be difficult to reconcile with the fourth of our terms of reference requirements – 'the maintenance of a link between MPs and geographical constituencies'. The Commission therefore does not feel that it can recommend STV in its full form as the best alternative to FPTP to be put before the people in a referendum.

Chapter Seven: The Case For and the Functioning of a Mixed System

108.   What system do we think may better fulfil our four reference requirements and our additional two tests? If we do not go in an STV direction the alternative must be a variant of the Additional Member System (henceforth AMS). As was previously expounded (paras 55-61) this has worked very well in Germany for half a century. What we propose for Britain is however substantially different from the German system both practically and conceptually. The practical differences are such that it may indeed be better to describe it for reasons which will emerge later as AV with Top-up members rather than AMS, although the two, while distinct, are recognisably of the same broad family. The conceptual differences arise from a contrast of origins. The modern German system stems from the old strict proportionality of the Weimar Republic and proceeds by substantial modification (a threshold of 5% to avoid a multiplicity of splinter parties, an obligation upon a Bundestag which defeats a government to provide another one in its place before the vote of no confidence is valid, etc.) in order successfully to avoid the governmental weakness of Weimar. Our proposition for this country stems essentially from the British constituency tradition and proceeds by limited modification to render it less haphazard, less unfair to minority parties, and less nationally divisive in the sense of avoiding large areas of electoral desert for each of the two major parties.

General Advantages of a Mixed System

109.   A principal advantage of such a mixed system is its flexibility. According to the proportion of top-up members which is fixed upon, and according somewhat also to whether they are elected nationally, or from big regions, or from a more local grouping of constituencies, varying degrees of priority can be given to proportionality on the one hand and to the constituency link on the other. This flexibility has enabled the Commission to steer to a point closest to fulfilling all four of our terms of reference, which, as well as greater proportionality and the maintenance of a constituency link, are an increase in voter choice and stability of government.

110.   The essence of the system is that the elector would have the opportunity to cast two votes, the first for his choice of constituency MP, the second for an additional or Top-up member who would be elected for the specific and primary purpose of correcting the disproportionality left by the constituency outcomes, and could thus be crucial to determining the political colour of the next government. The second vote can be cast either for individuals or (as in Germany) for a party list without regard to the individuals on it. For reasons we develop in paragraphs 137-9 we greatly prefer an 'open list', giving the voter the ability to discriminate between individuals, to a closed party list. The counting of the second votes must be done in such a way that the central purpose of the 'Top-up', which is leverage towards proportionality, is maintained. This means that account must be taken, not only of how many second votes a party has received, but also of how many constituency seats in the area it has already won. The allocation of Top-up seats would proceed as follows:

(i)   After the total number of second votes cast for each party have been counted, these numbers are then divided for each party by the number of constituencies gained in the

Top-up area by that party plus one (adding one avoids the impossibility of dividing by zero and ensures that the party with the highest ratio of votes to seats receives the Top-up seat.)

(ii) A Top-up member is then allocated to the party with the highest adjusted number of votes.

(iii) Where there remains a further Top-up member to be allocated this process is repeated but taking into account any Top-up members already gained by each party.

Parties should not be eligible for Top-up seats unless they have contested at least 50% of the constituencies in the Top-up area.

111.   Voter choice is manifestly enhanced by the ability of electors under the new system to cast their two votes in different political directions and thus to escape from the dilemma outlined earlier that, under FPTP, they have either to subordinate their view of who is the individual candidate best for the constituency to their choice of government for the country, or (less frequently in practice as all the evidence shows) *vice versa*. Thus, to take a concrete example, many Conservative voters of the Tatton division would at the last election have been able to balance their vote for the Labour and Liberal-supported independent candidate by using their second vote for a Conservative additional member from Cheshire. Martin Bell would still have been elected, but natural Conservatives could have eased the strain of a vote for him being a vote against John Major.

112.   From the point of view of stability of government there is no evidence that an additional member system, even in the extreme form of a 50:50 division between them and the constituency members, as practised in Germany, produces less stability of government than does FPTP. Furthermore there is no electoral system which is a guarantee against occasional periods of instability, as witness the already-cited FPTP results in Britain in 1922–4, 1950–51 and 1974. And, to cast the net of comparison wider, 'majoritarian' systems (very similar in effect to FPTP) have produced in France several periods of *co-habitation* (a government of a different political orientation from the President) and in the United States of a President with a hostile Congress.

113.   The Commission has therefore seen the essence of its task as being to use the flexibility of a Top-up system to strike such a balance as best to reconcile the four requirements of our terms of reference with our view of fairness, both of representation and of proportionality of power (as set out in paragraphs 6–8), and to do so in a way which offers a reasonable chance of our work being fecund rather than sterile.

The Status of MPs in a Mixed System

114.   AMS or its variants involves electing MPs by two different methods, and thus having, as some might put it, two classes of MPs. This is however unavoidable, unless either the search for greater fairness (and rationality) is to be abandoned or a solution is to be sought through universal STV or having all members elected on a list system, both of which solutions the Commission believes would be less acceptable.

115.   Some (mainly politicians) have raised the perceived problem of two categories of MPs. We do not see this problem as formidable. In the first place it is not really such a break with the British tradition as may superficially be thought. Throughout the nineteenth century there was a considerable difference of category between county and borough members. In addition the Scottish and Irish members were mostly elected on a different franchise from the English and Welsh ones. And some constituencies were always regarded, at any rate by some politicians, as having a greater prestige than others. Some saw the City of London as being peculiarly appropriate for great financiers or, on two occasions, for party leaders, and Lord Randolph Churchill several times tried to escape from what he regarded as the mediocrity of South Paddington to the romance of a 'great industrial borough'. The university seats, different both in electorate and in electoral method, persisted until 1950. And we are about to move into a position in which some MPs will represent areas with devolution and hence will have more restricted constitutency duties. Furthermore there has long been a difference of practice, if not of theory, between those who entered Parliament primarily to seek a national role, often switching from one constituency to an utterly disparate one in order to achieve it, and those who sprang out of a particular locality, found their greatest satisfaction in representing and serving it, and could not easily have been imagined, by themselves or others, as migrating to a seat in a different part of the country.

116.   A major disadvantage of the German system, if transported wholesale to Britain is that there would be too many list members. There is the equivalent of one list member for every constituency, and as many of them aspire to become directly elected constituency MPs, they concentrate their hopes and effort upon a particular constituency, in effect making themselves a shadow member for it, but with the substantial advantage over an adopted parliamentary candidate that they have all the advantages − access to ministers, full parliamentary expenses and salaried time when the Bundestag is not sitting − of the directly elected MP but without the constituency responsibility. By the criterion of a level playing field for the next elections this may be fair, but it is also inimical to the best traditions of an MP performing at least a semi-impartial role in his or her constituency between elections and endeavouring to serve all constituents − those who supported him or her and those who did not − with equal diligence. If there is a rival and equally active MP of an opposing party on the scene this link is almost inevitably weakened if not broken.

117.   Another disadvantage of such a high proportion of list members − to be set against the highly proportional outcomes which it secures − is that, particularly in scattered rural areas and doubly so if more rigid equity in constituency populations is sought, it loosens the local link. Apart from more extreme examples in Scotland and Wales, it would mean, to take a specific example from a fairly populous county of England, that there would only be one seat for the whole of north and west Devon stretching from Tavistock to Ilfracombe. And there is a third, and to many the principal disadvantage of a 50% 'top-up', which is that it would make coalitions if not inevitable very much the norm.

Proportionality and Stable Government

118.   It therefore appears to us that anything like 50% of Top-up members is undesirable. Fortunately it is also unnecessary. Studies done for the Commission show that a substantial degree of proportionality could be obtained for the country as a whole with a top-up of 15-20%.

119.   The next and central question which arises is why it is substantial proportionality and not complete proportionality that we are seeking. This necessarily flows from our terms of reference which require us to balance four competing criteria, of which broad proportionality is only one. We are required to steer a path which, so far as possible, reconciles this with the other three criteria.

120.   These external constraints are re-inforced by the consensual view of the Commission on the future political framework which we regard as desirable in itself and most likely to be acceptable to a majority of the British people in a referendum. As argued in Chapter 4 we do not recoil with horror from the very idea of coalitions, regarding them, on the basis both of British and of some foreign experience, as capable of providing effective and decisive governments. Their quality depends to some considerable extent on whether the coalitions are 'honest', defined in the sense that those within them agree with each other more than they do with those outside (sometimes indeed they may agree more than do those within single-party governments), rather than mere patchworks of opportunism.

121.   This does not mean that permanent coalition is desirable. We would prefer, and certainly regard as more compatible with the totality of our terms of reference, that when there is a strong surge in one political direction or the other, single-party governments, even if with somewhat under 50% of the vote, should stand out like mountainous land masses rising above the surface of the ocean. This should clearly have been the case with the Attlee government in 1945 and with the Macmillan government in 1959. No purpose of justice or efficacy would have been served by either being forced to coalesce with the very small Liberal party of those years.

122.   The position becomes more complicated with the decline of the two-party duopoly from 1974. Clearly in these past 24 years when governments found it easier to get big majorities with substantially lower percentages of the vote, any reformed system would have involved some coalitions. Particularly in 1974–9 and in 1992–7 they may well have been healthier for effective and responsive government. Nevertheless we would not wish to propound a system which would involve persistent coalition. Reverting to the comparison made with the German system, one aspect which we find difficult to defend, in spite of the striking overall economic and political success of German government, has been the permanent hinge position of the very small Free Democratic Party. In spite of having a voting strength on average barely a third of that of Alliance/Liberal Democrats since 1983, it was continuously in office from 1969 to 1998, with a perpetual grip on the Foreign Ministry and of two or three other cabinet seats as well. The pattern is being unfrozen by the rise of the Green party, which has recently moved to working inside rather than outside the system, and which in alliance with the SPD has excluded the FDP from the next government.

123.   Nevertheless, such a period of 29 years of almost guaranteed continuous if subsidiary power, for thirteen years with one ally, for sixteen years with another, obtained with an average of 8.7% (down to 6.2% at this year's election) of the vote seems to us to be an anomaly comparable (in the opposite direction) with the SDP/Liberal Alliance receiving only 3.5% of the seats for 25.4% of the vote in the 1983, or the Conservatives winning, mostly with big

majorities, four consecutive elections with an average of only 42.6% of the vote. The Commission does not wish to design such a position of constant privilege for a hinge party, and it does not believe there is anything inherent in an additional member/Top-up system which makes it do so.

124.   The Commission believes that it can iron out the gross anomalies, such as the Conservative and allied landslide of 1931, when a loss by Labour of 7% of the vote meant that it was deprived of 83% of its seats, or of Labour in February 1974, *per contra*, securing the right to form an independent government with only 37.2% of the votes, and fewer moreover than those of the Conservatives, without producing any likelihood of a stagnant and unhealthy prospect of constant and unchangeable coalition. That is how it sees its mandate of *greater* proportionality accompanied by respect for the other criteria.

Method of Electing Constituency Members

125.   A further question to be determined is whether, within an Additional Member/Top-up scheme, constituency MPs should be elected by FPTP or by AV. AV, it will be recalled, was shown in paragraph 81 as having many advantages, not least that it clearly increases voter choice (point iii of our terms of reference) and that it counteracts the growing tendency for many MPs to be elected by a plurality and not a majority of their constituents. To re-inforce the point made at paragraph 36 no fewer than 312 of the present 659 Members of the House of Commons were elected with less than 50% of the vote and of those 49 were elected with less than 40%.

126.   Under our system, AV would have a number of positive features which persuade a majority of us that it would be superior to FPTP as a method of choosing constituency representatives. First, there will be many fewer 'wasted votes' in the constituency side of the election, and far more voters will potentially influence the result. This, we hope, will encourage turn-out and participation. Second, it would encourage serious candidates to pitch their appeal to a majority of their constituents, rather than just seeking to target a hard-core minority of the party faithful. This should lead to more inclusive politics than FPTP. Third, because second and subsequent preferences may count, it will discourage individual candidates from intemperate attacks on their rivals, since they will be hoping to gain their second votes and will not wish to alienate their supporters. This should contribute to the more consensual and less confrontational politics to which the majority of the public appear to aspire.

127.   On top of these arguments, the use of AV has one other and crucial advantage. AV counters one important objection to electoral reform. This is the tendency to transfer power from voters to the subsequent deals of politicians. The recent example of New Zealand is widely cited in this regard. New Zealand is an example of the potential disadvantage of using FPTP for constituency elections under a mixed-system. For using FPTP means that each party in each constituency will seek to confront all others in order to maximise its own seats in the election, doing any necessary deals only after the polls have closed. By contrast, the use of AV in constituencies militates strongly against this.

128.   There can be an element of chance about individual constituency outcomes under AV, as there can be under almost all systems but it is probably less than that which exists under FPTP once tactical voting has become a factor, as it recently has in Britain. Those Conservative MPs who at the last election were faced by a clear leading challenger, whether it was a Labour or Liberal Democrat one, tended to lose their seats. Those who faced almost evenly divided opposition held them. That is a real example of randomness. Nor in our view is AV too complex for voters. AV is widely used in voluntary elections from the Church Synod to many local societies, and is widely understood.

129.   On its own, AV, which we also noted had the advantage that it could be implemented quickly without any change to constituency boundaries, was rejected on the ground that in the circumstances of 1997 (and maybe of the next election) it would be unfair to those who support the Conservative party, and that it is particularly important that parties in adversity should not be treated unfairly. It is also important to remember that in 1983, 1987 and 1992 AV would have brought no similar benefit to the Labour party over the Conservative party,

130.   The duty of the Commission, however, is to design a system which is of validity not just for the last or even the next election alone but for a much longer timespan. This gains particular force if the election after next, because of the burden placed upon the Boundary Commission by the need to reduce by approximately a fifth the number of constituencies, is the earliest point at which there is a realistic chance of our recommendations coming into operation. While we regret that there cannot be an earlier implementation we feel that by then the salient force of the 1997 election, which was the over-riding desire to end the long period of Conservative government, and which may also have some residual force at the next election of 2001 or 2002, must surely have expended itself.

131.   This, in combination with the still more important corrective mechanism of the Top-up, removes the decisive objection to AV on its own, which was its potential short-term unfairness to Conservative party supporters. In these circumstances the general view of the Commission is that the arguments outlined above swing in favour of AV for the constituencies. To sum up, AV extends voter choice while FPTP limits it. AV will substantially reduce the numbers of wasted votes because voters will be able to influence outcomes through second and sometimes third preferences and thus correct one of the mischiefs of the current system which is effectively to disenfranchise voters whose first preference is for small parties or independent candidates. And AV also guarantees that MPs are elected by a majority of those who vote in their constituencies, which majority is thereby given a stake in the validity of the representation. Lord Alexander has strong doubts about AV, and sets out his reasons, which are both conceptual and practical, in the attached note of reservation. He makes clear, however, that he supports wholly the recommendation of a 'top-up' with a great majority of constituency members but he considers that those members should continue as at present to be elected under FPTP.

Electing Top-up Members: A Local Solution

132.   The next issue is the geographical basis on which the list members should be allocated. We have wished to do this on a basis which is at once devolved and pays regard to historic local

entities. We propose that for the whole of the United Kingdom there should be 80 Top-up areas. Two of them would be in Northern Ireland (see para 141 below for our recommendation that under the AV plus system Northern Ireland would not require a different system), eight in Scotland and five in Wales. In the case of these latter two countries there has already been an allocation of Top-up areas for use in the elections to the Scottish Parliament and the Welsh Assembly. We see no reason to complicate the position by departing from these.

133.   This would leave 65 Top-up areas for England. What follows is offered for illustrative purposes. Outside the metropolitan areas we propose that these should be the "preserved" counties, although with the four largest in population – Kent, Essex, Lancashire and Hampshire – each split into two. London might be split into seven Top-up areas, conforming as far as possible to borough boundaries. In the ten other metropolitan areas of England there would be sixteen Top-up areas. In South Yorkshire, for instance, there might be the two Top-up seats of Sheffield with Rotherham and Barnsley with Doncaster. In West Yorkshire there might be three: one for Leeds, one for Bradford with Halifax, and one for the remaining urban areas comprising the towns of Huddersfield, Wakefield and Dewsbury. The full illustrative list, not only for England, but for Scotland, Wales and Northern Ireland is appended. All these 80 (in the UK) areas would have at least one Top-up member. The more populous ones and both Top-areas in Northern Ireland would have two. Where the dividing line is placed clearly depends on the exact proportion of Top-up seats which is thought desirable, and this is dealt with later in paragraphs 151–161.

134.   The strong advantage, as it appears to the Commission, of this devolved county/city allocation is (i) that its would help to restore some cohesion of representation to the recently weakened traditional localities of Britain; and (ii) that one or two additional members locally anchored to quite small areas comprising a maximum of 12 and an average of eight current constituencies put together are, we believe, more easily assimilable into the British political culture and indeed the Parliamentary system than would be a flock of unattached birds clouding the sky and wheeling under central party directions.

The Role of Top-up Members

135.   It is highly desirable that they should not be perceived as second grade MPs. It will of course continue to be for the members elected for constituencies to represent those constituencies at Westminster. We see the Top-up members as serving a new role in representing in the House of Commons the broader interests of the counties and cities. Top-up members will widen the opportunity for and access to parliamentary representation in two ways. It will be open to Top-up members at Westminster to represent the interests of their wider constituency on the hinge between the local authorities areas and Whitehall. And without prejudice to this broad responsibility to the wider constituency, the existence of Top-up members at county and city level across the country will provide representation in Parliament for minority political opinion, which because of the existence of electoral deserts created by the existing system, is currently extruded from large swathes of the country. The scope and breadth of these responsibilities should be such as to give to MPs elected as Top-up members fully equal status in the House of Commons to that of those elected in a constituency.

136.   Top-up or additional members are strongly likely to come from a spread of parties. Had the 1997 election been fought under our recommended system, for instance, there would have been more Conservative than Liberal Democrat Top-up members returned. Obviously when a party does as well in direct constituency elections as the Labour party then did there is not much scope for them to receive Top-up members as well. Even so they would have gained a few in the southern counties and at a more normally balanced election this few would have been considerably increased.

137.   While we do not think Top-up candidates should be legally prevented from simultaneously fighting individual constituencies (or *vice versa*), even more strongly do we feel that it should not be obligatory upon them to do so, nor indeed desirable. For this reason, amongst others, we differ from one of the recommendations of the admirable report of the Hansard Commission on Electoral Reform of 1976. This Commission was set up under the auspices of the Hansard Society and the chairmanship of the Conservative constitutional historian Lord Blake, with a distinguished membership including the then Chairman of ICI (Sir Jack Callard), Professor Ralf Dahrendorf, Lord O'Neill of the Maine, Baroness Seear and Richard Wood MP. It recommended an Additional Member System, and we have been much influenced by its powerfully presented argument. We differ however from its subsidiary proposal that list members should be chosen from the 'best losers'. We think that the concept of losers being transformed into winners, like base metal into gold, would not be an easy one to explain. Furthermore, the proportionally corrective function of additional members cannot always be performed by choosing 'best losers'. The second or third 'best loser' would quite often have to be chosen. And beyond that it would make a constituency contest obligatory for any additional member. We are in favour of greater flexibility on this last point.

Voter Choice

138.   Under a reformed system it is crucial that the voters' right to express their view of individual candidates should be at least maintained and preferably enhanced. FPTP does retain the right, theoretical in most cases but occasionally practical as the last election showed, to get rid of a deeply distasteful candidate even in a nominally safe seat. It would be a count against a new system if any candidate, by gaining party machine endorsement for being at the head of a list, were to achieve a position of effective immunity from the preference of the electorate. This is the essence of the case for open as opposed to closed lists for Top-up members.

139.   The practical importance of the issue can be exaggerated under a Top-up system as devolved as that which we propose. If there is in most cases no more than one Top-up seat for which to compete, and in no case more than two, parties are unlikely at the maximum to put forward a top-up list of more than three. That it should slightly exceed the number of seats available is desirable in order to provide for list vacancies between general elections, which will be dealt with in paragraph 143. Nevertheless it remains essential that the elector should have two rights; first to bolt the party ticket completely with his or her second vote, in other words to vote for a candidate of one party for the constituency and then to cast his or her vote in a different direction for the Top-up representative or representatives. Without this right the new system would not fulfil the objective of freeing the voter from the prison of having to

suffer an unwanted candidate for the constituency in order to get a desired government. Second, however, it is equally desirable that the voter should be able to discriminate between the candidates put forward for the list by the party for which he or she wishes to cast the second vote. Only if this is so does the Commission feel that it will have sufficiently discharged its third requirement of providing for an extension of voter choice.

140.   Equally, however, it should be recognised that all electors will not always wish to discriminate between candidates of the same party, perhaps for the very good reason that they know nothing about either or any of them. Where this is so a meaningless choice should not be enforced and the ticking of a party box should be an option. The desirability of freedom of choice is not invalidated by the fact that not everybody wishes to exercise it.

141.   Such freedom does involve a more complicated ballot paper than would be necessary under a more party-dominated system. If the right of the voter to split votes between constituency and list choices were eliminated only a single vote need be cast, with its consequence following through to determine the Top-up as well as the constituency result, and with the ballot paper looking exactly the same as in a FPTP election. But to abrogate a right to differentiate which 37% of New Zealanders and 12½% of Germans have chosen to exercise would be an unacceptable and unnecessary piece of caucus authoritarianism. In the same way the absence of choice between individual list candidates within a party would also somewhat simplify the ballot paper. Freedom always comes at a price, but this in our view is one which is worth paying. A typical sample ballot paper, assuming five parties, the average number of candidates for a constituency at the last election, is at Annex B.

Northern Ireland

142.   In recommending an alternative voting system for Westminster it was clearly essential for the Commission to be confident that it could be applied with equal validity throughout the United Kingdom. Our attention focused particularly on Northern Ireland where the political landscape differs in a number of ways from the rest of the United Kingdom. We found no sufficient case for recommending a different system for Northern Ireland. We were much persuaded to this view by the evidence submitted to us by the Northern Ireland Forum for Political Dialogue, and in particular the main conclusion of the Northern Ireland Committee on Electoral Reform that, while they hoped for a recommendation in favour of STV (as already used in Northern Ireland for local elections, elections to the European Parliament and the Assembly) it would in any event be preferable that the same system should be applied for parliamentary elections throughout the United Kingdom. Such uniform application we recommend, subject only to a special provision that there should be a minimum of four Top-up members (divided between two Top-up areas) for Northern Ireland. We believe this is necessary to accommodate the more complex party system which there operates.

By-Elections

143.   By-elections for constituency seats under the recommended system present no problems. They will be fought exactly as they are today except for the substitution of AV for FPTP. Where vacancies occur for Top-up MPs the position is more complicated, but it is

hardly a major issue, for it would be surprising if more than two or three such vacancies were to occur throughout the country in the course of a parliament. Election to a representative position should wherever possible be preferred to selection but it is difficult to see how one could be made to work in these rare circumstances. If a straight city or county-wide contest were to take place it would almost by definition result in the victory of the predominant party in the area, thus negating the essential purpose of the Top-up seats. If a highly complicated formula were evolved by which an election could take place but the results were adjusted so as to prevent this negation the outcome would suffer all and more of the disadvantages of turning best (or second or third best) losers into winners. In these isolated cases we therefore recommend that the next candidate on the Top-up list should move up. If for any reason there is no available person in this position the seat should remain vacant until the next general election.

Thresholds

144.   Is a threshold necessary in order to deter the securing of Top-up seats by very small splinter parties such as has tended to discredit the Israeli and the previous Italian systems? They of course are or were full list systems and thus very different from the limited Top-up which we are advocating. Nevertheless it has generally been accounted a favourable aspect of the German system that it has required a party to secure either 5% of the total vote or success in their direct constituency elections before it can qualify for any Top-up seats. This has been an effective safeguard against the fissiparousness of the system prevailing under the ill-fated Weimar Republic, although 5% necessarily has an arbitrary quality about it. Nonetheless if we believed that a threshold was necessary to prevent the evils of excessive splintering, we would certainly propose one. But all the indications are that it is unnecessary. At the last election under our highly devolved system with no more than one or two list seats for an area the lowest percentage of the total vote which would have placed a party in likely contention for a Top-up seat would have been the 10.9% scored by the Liberal Democrats in Nottinghamshire. As no-one could reasonably advocate a threshold nearly as high as that it would be a classic example of imposing an otiose constraint. We do not therefore recommend a formal threshold; our system itself imposes an informal one more severe than the Germans' 5%.

Tactical Voting

145.   Before we come to estimating the likely effects of the new system it is necessary to discuss one count against it which has been raised in advance. This is that it offers scope for tactical voting on a scale which would damage both the greater proportionality of the new system and its ability to counteract the "electoral deserts" for major parties scenario. Thus, to take an extreme case, Labour voters in Glasgow, knowing that because of their party's constituency dominance, it would have no chance of winning a compensating Top-up seat, might on a massive scale switch their Top-up vote to the Liberal Democrats, thereby depriving the Conservatives, whose real strength across the city is stronger than that of the Liberal Democrats, of the Top-up seat to which they should be entitled. It is easily possible to see the theory of the argument. The Commission, however, having examined it carefully, believe that its practical effects can be grossly exaggerated. Its comments on the issue follow in the next five paragraphs.

146.   All electoral systems are open to a degree of tactical voting. This is certainly true of
FPTP, where tactical voting was fairly widely practised in the special circumstances of the 1997
election, as was expounded in paragraph 128. There is nothing morally wrong about either
informal tactical voting or the formalisation of alternative choices under AV. In many
situations of life a decision has to be made in favour of a second or third best choice and there is
no inherent reason why what has often to be applied to jobs, houses, even husbands and wives
should be regarded as illegitimate when it comes to voting. The point at issue is the narrower
one of whether with an Additional Member/Top-up system tactical voting can block the
objective of the corrective mechanism giving greater proportionality.

147.   However the evidence is that effective tactical voting is very much a minority
occupation. Not much more than one in ten voters attempts it, and a much smaller proportion
achieve the result they intend. To suggest against this background that under a new system and
in the fog of battle which accompanies an election, parties are going to be able to manoeuvre
their votes, not in their own favour but in favour of another party, with all the precision of
guards' battalions on a parade-ground, seems to us distinctly far-fetched.

148.   For this to happen three unlikely conditions would have to be met. First, each party
with votes to spare would need to find and convey to its supporters a complete and fairly
precise confidence in the outcome before it had taken place. In retrospect the result of the 1997
election looks one of the most certain in living memory. Yet there was much nervousness and
uncertainty of mood in the Labour party during the campaign, just as there was in the
Conservative party (to which eloquent testimony is paid in the memoirs of the three members
of the high command at the time) in the run-up to the almost equally inevitable 1987 victory.
This is what is meant by the 'the fog of battle'. Second, the properties and likely result of a new
and somewhat more complicated system would have to be understood and foreseen with a
clinical precision which has rarely been associated with the old familiar system. And third, the
orders based on this precise appreciation would have to command the obedience not just of
militant cadres but of a somewhat inchoate mass of voters.

149.   Any reformed system is likely to be attacked by its opponents on the ground of
complications which will confuse the voters. This in our view is not a valid point, as is shown
by the much higher turnout in, for example, Germany in September, 1998 as compared with
the very low turnout under the simplifications of the United States' system. But also to claim
that it will be subject to the most sophisticated manipulation not only by party organisers but
the voters themselves is surely a classic example of trying to have it both ways.

150.   Furthermore the indications are that the maximum probable amount of tactical
vote-splitting would have been unlikely to make the results less proportional in 1997, and in
the more normal conditions of 1992 would have made it distinctly more proportional. There
may, compatibly with this, be some mild adverse effect upon a party which gets itself into as
unelectable a position as the Conservatives did in 1997 (and the Labour party in 1983), but it is
difficult with most electoral systems, certainly including FPTP, wholly to protect a party
against the consequences of such positions.

The Number of Top-up Members

151.   We now come to the next crucial question of what should be the size of the Top-up, and the best, but not necessarily certain, estimates which we can make (on the basis of psephological advice) of what likely results this combination of AV and limited Top-up would have produced for 1992 and 1997. We also give an indication of what might have been the 1983 and 1987 outcomes although it must be appreciated that the further back you go (rather in the way that the further forward a weather forecast goes) so the reliability of the estimates becomes less.

152.   In considering the level of Top-up we are required to balance carefully the potentially competing criteria set out in our terms of reference. On the one hand the importance of maintaining the link between MPs and their constituencies and the need to ensure stable government – to the arguable extent that this requires single party majority government most of the time – pushes towards keeping the level of Top-up as low as possible. On the other hand the requirement to deliver broad proportionality would push us towards a larger Top-up sufficient to correct, or at least substantially to ameliorate, potential disproportional outcomes on the constituency side.

153.   We were further constrained in our deliberations by the unavoidable reality that the political landscape in which we are operating is not static, and that, regrettably, we cannot realistically expect our recommendations to be in operation at a general election in much less than eight years. Changes to the landscape are already clearly visible on the horizon. Legislation to remove the statutory minimum for parliamentary constituencies in Scotland is currently before Parliament. This will inevitably result in a reduction in the number of the Scottish MPs at some point in the future – probably following the next Scottish Boundary Commission Review which is due to start in 2000. The level of over-representation in Wales is less dramatic but, in the wake of the creation of the Welsh Assembly, Parliament may want to address it as well. Furthermore it is impossible to judge the extent to which changes to the criteria which the Boundary Commission use for setting parliamentary boundaries, and which were the subject of criticism in an Home Affairs Select Committee Report in February 1987, can reduce the bias which, as we have described earlier, can affect different parties at different times, and which is currently working so forcefully against the Conservatives. A second stage of House of Lords reform is also clearly a strong possibility within the time-scale we are considering.

154.   This has not been an easy circle to square. We feel we can best do so by identifying a narrow range within which that level should be set in the light of developments outlined above. Our investigations (see Annex A) suggest that a Top-up of between 15% and 20% of MPs would do sufficient justice to the three competing criteria discussed above to be acceptable. It will be for Parliament to decide after the referendum (if favourable to change) on the basis of the evidence before it at the time at what point in that range the specific limit should be set. It will be crucial that the evidence provided to Parliament for this purpose is soundly-based, fair and demonstrably non-partisan. In our view this evidence would be best provided by an independent body such as an Electoral Commission. We discuss this in the context of the recent Neill Committee recommendations in paragraphs 166-168.

155.   For the sake of simplicity we think it best to give our estimates of the likely 1992 result under this recommended system at the middle point of the bracket, that is 17.5%. We obviously would not claim full precision for the exact numbers of seats which would have been won by each party, even though they have been arrived at with professional and impartial advice. We think it highly unlikely, however, that any margin of error for any party would exceed a handful of seats.

Table 2—1992 Election*

	CON	LAB	LIB DEM	SNP/PC	Various NI parties
FPTP	336	271	20	7	17
AV Top-up	316	240	74	11	18

*It should be noted that the projection prepared for the Commission superimposed 1992 voting patterns on to the scheme put forward by the Commission and therefore assume a House of Commons of 659 members.

156.   Instead of the weak and eroding Conservative majority which characterised the next five years, Mr Major would therefore have found himself from the start in a hung parliament, and a truly hung one, for a Labour/Liberal Democrats partnership would have been short of a majority, indeed just short of the Conservative total, and the Liberal Democrats had already moved to a sufficiently anti- Conservative position, not surprisingly perhaps after three Conservative parliaments, that a Major/Ashdown coalition, which could have commanded a majority, would have been impossible. The probable outcome would therefore have been an early second election, for which there have of course been several precedents under FPTP. It could easily be argued, however, that this might have been preferable from the point of view of decisive government than the five years of uncertain power which followed. It could also be argued that such an uncertain sound of the trumpet would have been a true reflection of the national mood in 1992 – a feeling that it was time for a change accompanied by a hesitation about entrusting power to the only partially reformed Labour party of the time, and that there is no need to apologise for an electoral system which would have accurately have reflected this uncertainty.

157.   On the same basis our estimates for the 1997 result are:

Table 3

	CON	LAB	LIB DEM	SNP/PC	Various NI parties	OTHER
FPTP	165	419	46	10	18	1
AV Top-up	168	368	89	15	18	1

158.   As will be seen this would not have prevented the Labour Party retaining a substantial overall majority of 77 – and one of 200 over the Conservatives – although it would of course have reduced the 'swollen' swing in seats. It would have substantially although not wholly eliminated the injustice to the Liberal Democrats (their strictly proportional entitlement was 111) and it would very marginally have improved the Conservative representation even at a time when their fortunes were nearly beyond the help of any electoral system.

159.   A further insight into the proportionality of our recommended system can be provided by the test of a statistical measuring rod known as a DV score, which measures the degree of deviation between a party's share of the vote and its share of seats. Again this rod does not have absolute validity but it is a useful indicator. Using this rod our researches show that when compared with FPTP our Top-up system reduced DV by one half (from 18 to 9) in 1992 conditions, and by just over one third (from 21 to 13. 2) in 1997 conditions. While these outcomes fall to a greater or lesser extent short of full proportionality (which, however, is generally considered to be achieved as fully as is normally practicable if the figure falls in the range of 4 to 8) this reflects our wish to minimise geographical disturbance and the prospect of constant coalition. The 1992 score also compares remarkably favourably with the outcome in the last Irish election, when their DV was actually higher at 9.8. The comparison is remarkable because STV (there operated) is generally considered by the most austere electoral reformers to be the epitome of desirability. It should however be noted that in the last but one Irish election the DV score was down to 6.8 and that in 1997 the British estimate is a good deal higher at 13.2. But 1997 in Britain was a 'bucking bronco' of an election which was very difficult for any system fully to control.

160.   Looking further back to 1983 and 1987 our own estimates are that our recommended system would on both occasions have produced overall Conservative majorities, of 30 in 1983 and 20 in 1987. Even allowing for a wider margin of error it is improbable that the governing party would have been overturned. These majorities, despite the Conservatives' vote shares in 1983 and 1987 being not very different from that achieved by the Labour party at the last election, would be considerably smaller than that of Labour in 1997. This must be in part due to the persistence of bias in any system largely founded on single member constituencies. The need to address this bias is integral to the successful implementation of our system (see paragraph 164).

161.   Our recommendation would therefore have produced single party majority Government in three out of the last four elections, with the only exception being a parliament which, even under the old system, exhibited many of the features of uncertain command. It is therefore difficult to argue that what we propose is a recipe either for a predominance of coalitions or for producing a weakness of government authority, except when it springs out of a hesitancy of national mood which may rightly show itself through any electoral system.

Chapter Eight: Related Issues

162.   The report so far has concentrated on tracing the Commission's path towards recommending an alternative voting system to be put to the public in a referendum. We now turn to important related issues, which, although not strictly within the Commission's terms of reference, bear significantly on the conduct of the referendum and implementation of the new system.

Boundary Commissions

163.   The role of the Boundary Commissions will be of key importance in implementing the voting system recommended in this report. There will be a need both to reduce the number of existing constituencies and to preserve the ratio of constituency to Top-up members. The Commission recommends that, both to ensure the stability of the ratio of constituency to Top-up members and to curb the tendency for the size of the House of Commons to creep up, the Boundary Commission should work to the present fixed number of MPs.

164.   Paragraphs 40 to 43 of this report identified the problem of bias under the existing system, two sources of which are the over-representation of Scotland and Wales and inequality of constituency size. We note that the Government has already undertaken that, in reviewing the distribution of seats in Scotland, the Boundary Commission will not be required to have regard to the existing statutory minimum number of seats for Scotland. It may be thought appropriate to correct the similar situation which exists in Wales. We also recommend that any changes to the Boundary Commissions' criteria have regard to the need to correct sources of bias, for example, by moving to the use of a single electoral quota for the United Kingdom as a whole. The nature of the Top-up system we recommend, which will require that constituencies follow the boundaries of counties and chosen metropolitan areas, will indeed place some further restriction on the flexibility of Boundary Commissions in achieving constituencies of equal size. We do, however, consider that the ability of the Boundary Commissions to prevent their work becoming quickly out of date would be assisted by the statutory power to take account of projections of population changes.

165.   We also recommend, in order to achieve the objectives set out above, that there be greater co-ordination of the work of the separate Boundary Commissions for England, Scotland, Wales and Northern Ireland and that this function should be entrusted to an Electoral Commission which we discuss in paragraph 167-8.

Oversight of Electoral Matters and Conduct of the Referendum

166.   In the course of the Commission's work, many compelling representations have been made of the need for independent oversight of electoral administration and related matters, and in particular of the conduct of referendums. The representations have without exception placed strong emphasis on the need for a publicly-funded (and therefore impartially informative rather than partisan) civic education programme to prepare the general public for the decision they would be asked to make in the referendum on the voting system which should follow this report.

167.   We make two particular recommendations. First, the oversight of elections and electoral administration generally should be undertaken independently of government by an Electoral Commission. Although our elections are generally free and fairly conducted the rules governing their administration and conduct are outdated, complicated and inefficient. The case for such a commission is made forcefully by Professor David Butler in the Hansard Society report "The Case for an Electoral Commission – Keeping Electoral Law Up-to-date" which was published in February 1998. We hope the Government will accept the Neill Committee's recommendation that such a body should be established, but we accept that this may not be in place in time to inform early decisions on the system resulting from this report. We believe that an Electoral Commission could play a crucial role in preparing for implementation of the new system and, in the longer term, in monitoring its practical impact and advising Government and Parliament on the need for any adjustment.

168.   Second, we strongly support the practical guidelines set down in the Report of the Commission on the Conduct of Referendums, chaired by Sir Patrick Nairne under the aegis of the Constitution Unit and the Electoral Reform Society. In particular we urge the Government to accept the recommendation, echoed by the Neill Committee, for an independent body to oversee the conduct of referendums, although we think that the Government should be entitled firmly to express its own view in any such referendum. It seems to us that an Electoral Commission would be best placed to discharge this role in relation to the referendum on the voting system. But if this is not in place we recommend that an independent Referendum Commission should be established to oversee the conduct of the referendum and, in the run up, the planning and oversight of the civic education programme, which we see as essential. It could also advise on the wording of the question. The success of the referendum could depend on the question being clear, simple and not open to legal challenge.

Arrangements for Reviewing the Electoral System

169.   Another point made forcefully to us by many of our interlocutors, particularly overseas, was the need for a review of the new electoral system after it has been in operation for a reasonable period. The Conservative party's submission to the Commission calls for a further referendum after 10 years. Without endorsing such an advance commitment we believe strongly that a review process is desirable. First, we believe that a commitment to a review will encourage the accumulation of evidence from practical experiences as the system settles down. And second, the certainty of an objective review after a set period of time will help to stabilise the system in its early years.

170.   We therefore recommend that a review should take place after, say, two general elections have taken place under the new system. Decisions as to the body responsible for conducting the review will be for the Government and Parliament. If, as we hope, an Electoral Commission has been established, that body would be in a position to offer useful advice on the arrangements for such a review, and maybe even conduct the review itself. We strongly recommend that fundamental change, such as substantially increasing or decreasing the ratio of Top-up members or a return to FPTP, should not be introduced without a further referendum.

Chapter Nine: Recommendations and Conclusions

1.   The Commission's central recommendation is that the best alternative for Britain to the existing First Past The Post system is a two-vote mixed system which can be described as either limited AMS or AV Top-up. The majority of MPs (80 to 85%) would continue to be elected on an individual constituency basis, with the remainder elected on a corrective Top-up basis which would significantly reduce the disproportionality and the geographical divisiveness which are inherent in FPTP.

2.   Within this mixed system the constituency members should be elected by the Alternative Vote. On its own AV would be unacceptable because of the danger that in anything like present circumstances it might increase rather than reduce disproportionality and might do so in a way which is unfair to the Conservative party. With the corrective mechanism in operation, however, its advantages of increasing voter choice and of ensuring that in practice all constituency members (as opposed to little more that half in recent elections) have majority support in their own constituencies become persuasive. Lord Alexander would, however, prefer to retain FPTP for constituency elections for the reasons outlined in the attached note.

3.   The Commission recommends that this system should be implemented throughout the United Kingdom.

4.   The Commission recommends that the second vote determining the allocation of Top-up members should allow the voter the choice of either a vote for a party or for an individual candidate from the lists put forward by parties. They should therefore be what are commonly called open rather than closed lists.

5.   The Commission recommends that, in the interests of local accountability and providing additional members with a broad constituency link, additional members should be elected using small Top-up areas. The Commission recommends the areas most appropriate for this purpose are the 'preserved' counties and equivalently sized metropolitan districts in England. In Scotland and Wales, we see no reason to depart from the units which are used for the return of additional members to the Parliament in Scotland and to the Assembly in Wales with respectively eight and five Top-up areas. In Northern Ireland there should be two Top-up areas each returning two members. In England the Top-up members would therefore in effect be either county or city-wide members from 65 different areas

6.   The Commission recommends that the Top-up members should be allocated correctively, that is on the basis of the second vote and taking into account the number of constituency seats gained by each party in each respective area, according to the following method:

- the number of second votes cast for each party will be counted and divided by the number of constituency MPs plus one gained by each party in each area;

- the party with the highest number of second votes after this calculation will be allocated the first Top-up member;
- any second additional member for an area will be allocated using the same method but adjusting to the fact that one party will already have gained a Top-up member.

7.   The Commission recommends that the proportion of Top-up members needed for broad proportionality without imposing a coalition habit on the country should be between 15% and 20%. A decision on the exact proportion of Top-up members should be governed by the considerations set out in paragraphs 151–154 of this report, which relate to other changes in the pipeline such as the reduction in the number of Scottish seats and the work of the Boundary Commissions.

8.   The Commission recommends that the allocation of Top-up seats to areas should ensure that the ratio of constituency to Top-up members is, as far as is practicable, equal in the four constituent nations of the United Kingdom. The allocation of Top-up members to the areas within each of those parts should ensure that each area has at least one Top-up member with the remainder being allocated to those areas with the greatest number of electors. For the reasons outlined in paragraph 142 Northern Ireland should have two Top-up members in two Top-up areas.

9.   The Commission recommends that the right to put forward candidates for Top-up member seats should be limited to those parties which have candidates standing for election in at least half of the constituencies within the the Top-up area.

10.   The Commission stresses that all members of the House of Commons whether elected from constituencies or as Top-up members should have equal status in Westminster.

11.   The Commission recommends that Top-up member vacancies, which are unlikely to be more than two or three a parliament, should be filled by the candidate next on the list of the party holding the seat. If there is no available person the seat should remain vacant until the next general election. Constituency vacancies would of course be filled by the normal by-election procedure.

12.   The Commission believes that changes to the existing Rules for the Redistribution of Seats (Schedule 2 to the Parliamentary Constituencies Act 1986) will be integral to the successful implementation of the new system. Bias should be reduced by the use of a single electoral quota for the United Kingdom; and the Boundary Commissions should be given a statutory power to take account of population movement and thus help to keep the result of their work more up-to-date.

Secondary Recommendations

13.   The Commission recommends that there should be a properly planned publicly-funded but neutrally-conducted education programme to prepare voters for the decision they will be required to make in the referendum.

14.   The Commission concludes that the education programme and oversight of referendums generally should fall to an independent commission. This role would fall naturally to an Electoral Commission.

15.   The Commission recommends that an independent Electoral Commission should be established to advise Parliament on and have oversight of electoral administration and related matters.

16.   The Commission recommends that the Government should put in place arrangements to review the new system after, say, two general elections.

17.   The Commission recommends that substantial further changes should not be made without a second referendum.

Note of Reservation by Lord Alexander

I support all but one of the recommendations in the Report. Whilst I agree with the main thrust of the proposal that an additional member or 'top-up' system is the best alternative to our existing electoral arrangements, I do not share the view of my colleagues that AV, rather than FPTP, is an appropriate way of electing constituency members.

This is not an arcane or technical issue primarily of interest to connoisseurs of electoral reform. Quite the contrary. The single member constituency will remain the linchpin of our electoral system, under which about 80% of members will be elected. So it is crucial that the method of election within these constituencies should be sound in principle, easy to understand and above all capable of commanding the enduring respect of the electorate. I do not consider that AV satisfies these tests.

My colleagues support AV because they think it important to ensure that every member gains some measure of majority support from the voters in their constituency. Yet most votes in constituencies are cast for a party, not an individual. Once an election is over, however, there is a long-standing tradition that MPs are available to serve all their constituents. MPs do not do this any less well where they have under 50% of the vote. Indeed they need to work hard to garner future support. This healthy convention diminishes the need for the party from which the member comes to have some form of support from a majority of voters in an individual constituency. In addition there will be MPs within the Top-up areas from parties previously unrepresented in those areas who will be available to any voters particularly wanting to consult an MP from their own party.

My colleagues also think that AV will contribute to a less confrontational style of politics because candidates will be inhibited from attacking rivals too strongly as they wish to gain their second votes. I do not see it as particularly desirable that candidates from different parties, who are different precisely because they do not agree on all issues, should be pulling their punches in order to seek approval from voters who support other parties. In any event, from my observation of Australia, which is the only single large country to use AV, their politicians tend to be, if anything, more blunt and outspoken than our own.

It has also been suggested that AV gives more power to voters and less to politicians. Under AV parties can advise their supporters how to cast their second preference votes so as to favour those parties with whom they might wish to go into coalition in the event of a hung parliament. This is said to have the potential desirable consequence that pre-election agreements as to coalitions, rather than post election negotiations, can be put before the voters. But this raises another concern. Whilst tactical voting is already an increasing feature of elections, AV could further heighten the tendency and lead to attempts by two parties to marshal their supporters so as to gang up on a third. This is precisely what those who are suspicious of electoral reform fear. I think that so far as AV is concerned this fear could prove to be well founded.

There was no groundswell of enthusiasm for AV in the submissions we received. The Conservative Party has consistently and clearly continued to express its support for the existing system. The Liberal Democrats have been equally constant in their support for STV under which no individual MP normally has majority support. The Electoral Reform Society also advocated STV. It is true that in the Plant Report SV (a slight variant of AV) was recommended, but the Labour Party has never endorsed this proposal. In its submission to us it expressed no view at all on what was the best electoral system, but highlighted criteria which pointed ambiguously towards either FPTP or AV.

I also regard it as significant that Parliament has very recently twice endorsed FPTP for constituency elections under a 'top-up' system for both the Scottish Parliament and the Welsh Assembly. So far as I am aware no one attempted to amend these proposals to introduce AV. To change to AV for Westminster elections would create an unjustified and confusing inconsistency between electoral systems for the United Kingdom Parliament and those two important institutions.

While I regard all these practical points as important, I also have a deep-rooted anxiety that AV cannot be regarded as sound or fair in principle.

AV comes into play only when a candidate fails to secure a majority of first preference votes. It does not, however, then take account of the second preferences of all voters, but only of those who have supported the least successful candidates. So it ignores the second preferences of the voters who supported the two candidates with the highest first preference votes, but allows the voters for the third or even weaker candidates to have their second votes counted so as to determine the result.

I find this approach wholly illogical. Why should the second preferences of those voters who favoured the two stronger candidates on the first vote be totally ignored and only those who support the lower placed and less popular candidates get a second bite of the cherry? Why, too, should the second preferences of these voters be given equal weight with the first preferences of supporters of the stronger candidates? In 1931 Mr Winston Churchill described this proposal as taking account of "the most worthless votes of the most worthless candidates". He went on to describe AV as containing an element of blind chance and accident which would lower respect for Parliament. Churchill's comments warrant even greater weight because at that time he was not unsympathetic to some sensible form of electoral reform.

In addition, as all experts on electoral systems have acknowledged, AV can operate haphazardly depending upon the ranking of candidates on first preference votes. David Butler and his expert colleagues drew attention to this in their advice to the Commission and deliberately gave a far-fetched illustration but I will try to demonstrate the point with a more homespun example.

Suppose within a constituency, Conservatives receive 40% of first preferences. Labour are second on 31% and Lib Dems third on 29%. Lib Dems second preferences happen to be split 15/14 in favour of Labour. The Conservatives are therefore elected with 54% of the total vote (i.e. 40% + 14%).

But now suppose the position of Labour and Lib Dems had been reversed on first preferences, with Lib Dems 31% and Labour 29%. If Labour second preferences were split 20/9 in favour of Lib Dems, the Lib Dems would be elected with 51% of the total vote (i.e. 31% + 20%).

So the result would be different depending on which horse was second and which third over Becher's Brook first time round. This seems to me too random to be acceptable.

I have one other concern about the use of AV in constituency elections. It is true that in most elections it would apparently have made little difference to the total number of seats gained by each party. But in elections where one main party is particularly unpopular it would punish that party disproportionately. It would have hurt Labour when they were clobbered by the voters in 1983 and similarly hurt the Conservatives in 1997. It would have treated these parties worse than under a 'top-up' system where constituency members are elected under FPTP. All of us take the view that parties in adversity should not be treated unfairly. This seems to me an additional argument for retaining FPTP for constituency elections within an additional member system.

In summary, I wholly support the recommendation for an additional member system. But I believe the constituency elections should be conducted under FPTP. This would involve only one change to our current electoral system. It would preserve the relationship between MPs and their constituents of all parties on the basis of a method of constituency election which is familiar. I believe that this single change would both achieve an extension of voter choice and a significant increase in proportionality with the minimum disruption to our current electoral system. It could be simply and powerfully presented to the electorate as leading to fairer representation of their votes both at Westminster and in the Top-up areas.

ANNEXES

ANNEX A

PROJECTED OUTCOMES OF 1992 AND 1997 ELECTIONS WITH BETWEEN USING AV TOP-UP WITH 15% AND 20% TOP-UP MEMBERS

Table 1: 20% or 132 Top-up members in 1997

	CON	LAB	LIB DEM	SNP/PC	NI Parties	OTHER	DV Score
FPTP	165	419	46	10	18	1	21
AV Top-Up	175	360	90	15	18	1	12

Table 2: 20% or 132 Top-up members in 1992

	CON	LAB	LIB DEM	SNP/PC	NI Parties	DV Score
FPTP	336	271	20	7	17	18
AV Top-Up	309	240	81	11	18	8.1

Table 3: 15% or 98 Top-up members in 1997

	CON	LAB	LIB DEM	SNP/PC	NI Parties	OTHER	DV Score
FPTP	165	419	46	10	18	1	21
AV Top-Up	160	378	88	14	18	1	14.8

Table 4: 15% or 98 Top-up members in 1992

	CON	LAB	LIB DEM	SNP/PC	NI Parties	DV Score
FPTP	336	271	20	7	17	18
AV Top-Up	315	244	71	11	18	9.5

FORMAT OF TWO-VOTE BALLOT PAPER

CONSTITUENCY VOTE

This vote will help to decide who is the constituency MP for Westbury. Rank the candidates in order of preference (1 for your preferred candidate, then 2, 3 etc.). Rank as many candidates as you wish.

	place the candidates in order of preference (1, 2, 3 etc)
Stephen Collins *Conservative*	
Candice Crosby *Liberal Democrat*	
Dennis Graham *Referendum Party*	
Stephanie Mills *Natural Law Party*	
Amina Mir *Independent*	
Diane Morgan *Labour*	
Martin Newman *Green Party*	
Peter Quine *Independent*	
Robert Russell *UK Independence Party*	

SECOND VOTE

This vote will help to decide the total number of seats for each party in the county of Purfordshire. You may vote either for one party or, if you wish, for one of the listed candidates. A vote for a listed candidate will also be counted as a vote for that candidate's party.

EITHER put an X against the party of your choice	OR put an X against the candidate of your choice
☐ Conservative	☐ Giles Anderson ☐ John Coleman ☐ Julia Smith
☐ Labour	☐ Helen Baxter ☐ Tom Franklyn ☐ Donna Jones
☐ Liberal Democrat	☐ Carol Newton ☐ Fazal Hussain ☐ Julian Morison
☐ Natural Law	☐ Paul Delaney ☐ Nasim Shah
☐ Referendum	☐ Anthony Barber ☐ Denise Docherty

		Local seats	Top-up seats	Total seats
SCOTLAND				
S1	Scotland Highlands	6	1	7
S2	Scotland North East	7	2	9
S3	Scotland Mid & Fife	8	1	9
S4	Scotland West	8	1	9
S5	Glasgow	8	2	10
S6	Scotland Central	8	2	10
S7	Lothians	7	2	9
S8	Scotland South	7	2	9
COUNTIES				
C1	Northumberland	3	1	4
C2	Cumbria	5	1	6
C3	Durham	6	1	7
C4	Cleveland	5	1	6
C5	Lancashire: North	6	1	7
C6	Lancashire: South	7	1	8
C7	North Yorkshire	7	1	8
C8	Humberside	8	2	10
C9	Cheshire	9	2	11
C10	Shropshire	4	1	5
C11	Staffordshire	10	2	12
C12	Derbyshire	8	2	10
C13	Nottinghamshire	9	2	11
C14	Leicestershire	8	2	10
C15	Lincolnshire	6	1	7
C16	Hereford & Worc.	7	1	8
C17	Gloucestershire	5	1	6
C18	Oxfordshire	5	1	6
C19	Warwickshire	4	1	5
C20	Northamptonshire	5	1	6
C21	Buckinghamshire	6	1	7
C22	Bedfordshire	5	1	6
C23	Cambridgeshire	6	1	7
C24	Hertfordshire	9	2	11
C25	Norfolk	6	2	8
C26	Suffolk	6	1	7
C27	Essex: North East	6	1	7
C28	Essex: South West	8	2	10
C29	Cornwall	4	1	5
C30	Devon	9	2	11
C31	Somerset	4	1	5
C32	Bristol and Bath	8	2	10
C33	Wiltshire	5	1	6
C34	Dorset	7	1	8
C35	Berkshire	7	1	8
COUNTIES (cont.)				
C36	Hampshire North	7	2	9
C37	Hampshire Solent	7	2	9
C38	Surrey	9	2	11
C39	West Sussex	7	1	8
C40	East Sussex	7	1	8
C41	Kent: West	9	2	11
C42	Kent: East	5	1	6
WALES				
W1	Wales North	7	2	9
W2	Wales Mid	7	1	8
W3	South Wales West	6	1	7
W4	South Wales Central	8	2	10
W5	South Wales East	7	1	8
METROPOLITAN COUNTIES				
M1	Tyne & Wear: N & Newc.	4	1	5
M2	Tyne & Wear: South	7	1	8
M3	Liverpool and Wirral	7	2	9
M4	Merseyside: North	6	1	7
M5	Manchester: East	8	2	10
M6	Manchester: West	7	2	9
M7	Manchester: North	7	2	9
M8	West Yorkshire: Bradford	6	1	7
M9	West Yorkshire: Leeds	7	1	8
M10	West Yorkshire: South	7	1	8
M11	South Yorkshire: Sheffield	8	1	9
M12	South Yorkshire: Barnsley	5	1	6
M13	Wolverhampton & Walsall	5	1	6
M14	Dudley and Sandwell	6	1	7
M15	Birmingham	9	2	11
M16	Coventry & Solihull	4	1	5
LONDON				
L1	North West London	9	2	11
L2	North London	9	2	11
L3	North Central London	9	2	11
L4	North East London	8	2	10
L5	South West London	7	2	9
L6	South Central London	9	2	11
L7	South East London	9	2	11
NORTHERN IRELAND				
N1	Northern Ireland East	8	2	10
N2	Northern Ireland West	6	2	8

AREAS FOR ELECTING TOP-UP MPs*

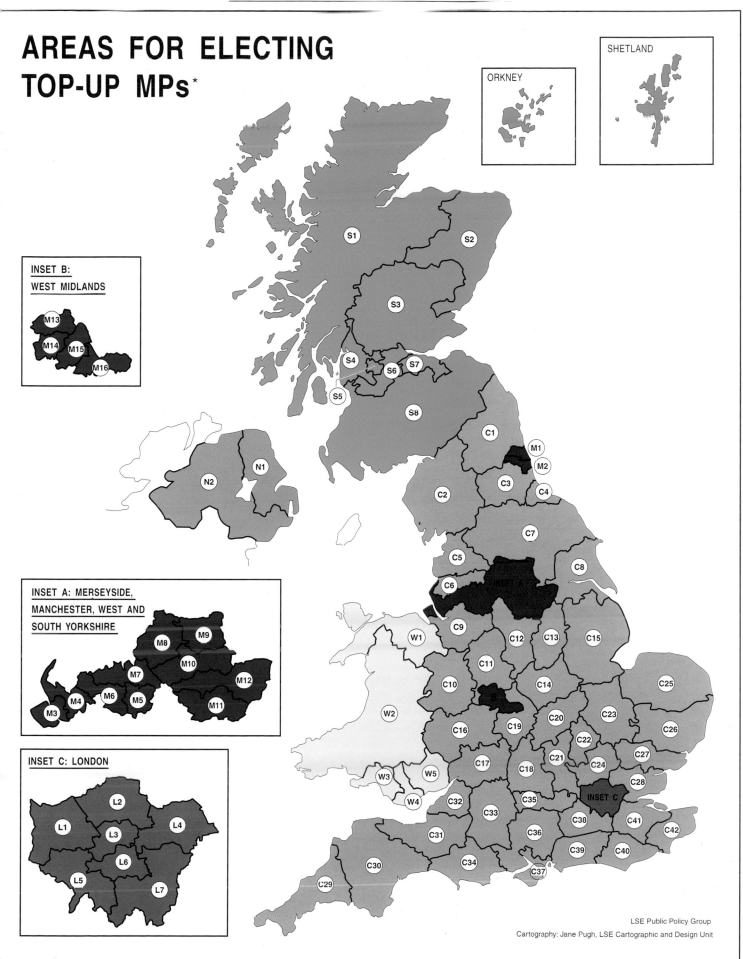

ORKNEY

SHETLAND

INSET B:
WEST MIDLANDS

INSET A: MERSEYSIDE,
MANCHESTER, WEST AND
SOUTH YORKSHIRE

INSET C: LONDON

LSE Public Policy Group

Cartography: Jane Pugh, LSE Cartographic and Design Unit

*This map is intended to be illustrative only

Illustrative list of current constituencies within Top-up areas.

Top Up Area			
No	Name		Current Constituencies Included

NORTH WEST

C	5	Lancashire: North	Lancaster & Wyre
			Morecambe & Lunesdale
			Fylde
			Ribble Valley
			Pendle
			Blackpool South
			Blackpool North & Fleetwood
C	6	Lancashire: South	Burnley
			Rossendale & Darwen
			Hyndburn
			Blackburn
			Ribble South
			Preston
			Chorley
			Lancashire West
C	9	Cheshire	Warrington North
			Warrington South
			Halton
			Weaver Vale
			Macclesfield
			Tatton
			Chester, City of
			Ellesmere Port & Neston
			Congleton
			Eddisbury
			Crewe & Nantwich
M	5	Manchester: East	Manchester, Blackley
			Manchester, Central
			Manchester, Gorton
			Manchester, Withington
			Hazel Grove
			Stalybridge & Hyde
			Stockport
			Cheadle
			Denton & Reddish
			Ashton under Lyne
M	6	Manchester: West	Wythenshawe & Sale East
			Altrincham & Sale West
			Stretford & Urmston
			Salford
			Eccles
			Worsley
			Leigh
			Wigan
			Makerfield
M	7	Manchester: North	Oldham West & Royton
			Oldham East & Saddleworth
			Heywood & Middleton
			Rochdale
			Bury South
			Bury North
			Bolton North East
			Bolton South East
			Bolton West

Top Up Area

No	Name	Current Constituencies Included
M 4	Merseyside: North	St Helens South
		St Helens North
		Crosby
		Southport
		Bootle
		Knowsley South
		Knowsley North & Sefton East
M 3	Liverpool and Wirral	Wirral West
		Wirral South
		Birkenhead
		Wallasey
		Liverpool, Walton
		Liverpool, West Derby
		Liverpool, Wavertree
		Liverpool, Garston
		Liverpool, Riverside
C 2	Cumbria	Westmorland & Lonsdale
		Barrow & Furness
		Copeland
		Workington
		Carlisle
		Penrith & The Border

NORTH EAST

No	Name	Current Constituencies Included
C 1	Northumberland	Blyth Valley
		Wansbeck
		Berwick-upon-Tweed
		Hexham
C 3	Durham	Bishop Auckland
		Durham North West
		Durham North
		Durham, City of
		Sedgefield
		Darlington
		Easington
M 1	Tyne and Wear: North and Newcastle	Tyneside North
		Tynemouth
		Newcastle upon Tyne North
		Newcastle upon Tyne East & Wallsend
		Newcastle upon Tyne Central
M 2	Tyne and Wear: South	Houghton & Washington East
		Gateshead East & Washington West
		Tyne Bridge
		Blaydon
		Jarrow
		South Shields
		Sunderland North
		Sunderland South
C 4	Cleveland	Redcar
		Hartlepool
		Stockton North
		Middlesbrough
		Middlesbrough South & East Cleveland
		Stockton South

YORKSHIRE AND HUMBERSIDE

No	Name	Current Constituencies Included
M 12	South Yorkshire: Barnsley and Doncaster	Barnsley West & Penistone
		Barnsley Central
		Barnsley East & Mexborough
		Don Valley
		Doncaster North
		Doncaster Central

Top Up Area			Current Constituencies Included
No		Name	
M	11	South Yorkshire: Sheffield and Rotherham	Wentworth
			Rother Valley
			Rotherham
			Sheffield, Central
			Sheffield, Hallam
			Sheffield, Hillsborough
			Sheffield, Brightside
			Sheffield, Attercliffe
			Sheffield, Heeley
M	10	West Yorkshire: South	Colne Valley
			Huddersfield
			Batley & Spen
			Dewsbury
			Pontefract & Castleford
			Hemsworth
			Normanton
			Wakefield
M	8	West Yorkshire: Bradford	Keighley
			Shipley
			Halifax
			Calder Valley
			Bradford South
			Bradford North
			Bradford West
M	9	West Yorkshire: Leeds	Leeds West
			Pudsey
			Leeds North West
			Leeds North East
			Elmet
			Leeds East
			Morley & Rothwell
			Leeds Central
C	8	Humberside	Hull East
			Beverley & Holderness
			Hull West & Hessle
			Hull North
			Yorkshire East
			Haltemprice & Howden
			Great Grimsby
			Cleethorpes
			Scunthorpe
			Brigg & Goole
C	7	North Yorkshire	York, City of
			Selby
			Harrogate & Knaresborough
			Vale of York
			Scarborough & Whitby
			Ryedale
			Skipton & Ripon
			Richmond (Yorks)

EAST MIDLANDS

C	12	Derbyshire	Bolsover
			Amber Valley
			Derbyshire North East
			Chesterfield
			Derbyshire West
			High Peak
			Derby North
			Derby South
			Erewash
			Derbyshire South

Top Up Area		
No	Name	Current Constituencies Included
C 13	Nottinghamshire	Newark
		Bassetlaw
		Mansfield
		Ashfield
		Nottingham South
		Broxtowe
		Nottingham North
		Nottingham East
		Sherwood
		Rushcliffe
		Gedling
C 14	Leicestershire	Loughborough
		Leicestershire North West
		Bosworth
		Charnwood
		Harborough
		Blaby
		Rutland & Melton
		Leicester South
		Leicester West
		Leicester East
C 20	Northamptonshire	Daventry
		Kettering
		Corby
		Wellingborough
		Northampton North
		Northampton South
C 15	Lincolnshire	Lincoln
		Gainsborough
		Sleaford & North Hykeham
		Grantham & Stamford
		South Holland & The Deepings
		Louth & Horncastle
		Boston & Skegness
	EASTERN	
C 25	Norfolk	Norwich North
		Norwich South
		Norfolk Mid
		Norfolk North
		Norfolk North West
		Norfolk South West
		Great Yarmouth
		Norfolk South
C 23	Cambridgeshire	Cambridgeshire North East
		Cambridgeshire North West
		Peterborough
		Huntingdon
		Cambridgeshire South
		Cambridgeshire South East
		Cambridge
C 26	Suffolk	Suffolk Central & Ipswich North
		Bury St Edmunds
		Suffolk South
		Suffolk West
		Ipswich
		Suffolk Coastal
		Waveney

Top Up Area			Current Constituencies Included
No		Name	
C	22	Bedfordshire	Bedfordshire North East
			Bedford
			Bedfordshire South West
			Bedfordshire Mid
			Luton North
			Luton South
C	24	Hertfordshire	Hitchin & Harpenden
			Stevenage
			Hertford & Stortford
			Hertfordshire North East
			Broxbourne
			Welwyn Hatfield
			Hemel Hempstead
			St Albans
			Hertfordshire South West
			Watford
			Hertsmere
C	27	Essex: North East	Saffron Walden
			Braintree
			Essex North
			Harwich
			Colchester
			Maldon & East Chelmsford
			Chelmsford West
C	28	Essex: South West	Harlow
			Epping Forest
			Rayleigh
			Castle Point
			Rochford & Southend East
			Southend West
			Brentwood & Ongar
			Billericay
			Thurrock
			Basildon

WEST MIDLANDS

M	13	Wolverhampton and Walsall	Walsall North
			Walsall South
			Aldridge - Brownhills
			Wolverhampton South East
			Wolverhampton North East
			Wolverhampton South West
M	16	Coventry and Solihull	Coventry South
			Coventry North East
			Meriden
			Coventry North West
			Solihull
M	15	Birmingham	Birmingham, Ladywood
			Birmingham, Perry Barr
			Birmingham, Hodge Hill
			Sutton Coldfield
			Birmingham, Erdington
			Birmingham, Yardley
			Birmingham, Sparkbrook & Small Heath
			Birmingham, Edgbaston
			Birmingham, Northfield
			Birmingham, Selly Oak
			Birmingham, Hall Green

Top Up Area		Current Constituencies Included
No	Name	
M 14	Dudley and Sandwell	West Bromwich West
		West Bromwich East
		Dudley South
		Dudley North
		Warley
		Stourbridge
		Halesowen & Rowley Regis
C 11	Staffordshire	Stoke-on-Trent North
		Staffordshire Moorlands
		Stoke-on-Trent Central
		Newcastle-under-Lyme
		Stoke-on-Trent South
		Stone
		Burton
		Tamworth
		Lichfield
		Cannock Chase
		Staffordshire South
		Stafford
C 10	Shropshire	Shropshire North
		Shrewsbury & Atcham
		Wrekin, The
		Telford
		Ludlow
C 16	Hereford and Worcester	Worcestershire Mid
		Wyre Forest
		Hereford
		Leominster
		Worcestershire West
		Worcester
		Bromsgrove
		Redditch
C 19	Warwickshire	Warwick & Leamington
		Rugby & Kenilworth
		Stratford on Avon
		Warwickshire North
		Nuneaton
	SOUTH EAST	
C 36	Hampshire North	Aldershot
		Hampshire North East
		Hampshire North West
		Basingstoke
		Winchester
		Romsey
		Hampshire East
		New Forest East
		New Forest West
C 37	Hampshire Solent	Southampton, Itchen
		Southampton, Test
		Fareham
		Eastleigh
		Gosport
		Isle of Wight
		Portsmouth South
		Portsmouth North
		Havant

| Top Up Area | | Current Constituencies Included |
No	Name	
C 39	West Sussex	Bognor Regis & Littlehampton
		Chichester
		Crawley
		Horsham
		Worthing West
		Worthing East & Shoreham
		Arundel & South Downs
		Sussex Mid
C 40	East Sussex	Brighton, Pavilion
		Brighton, Kemptown
		Hove
		Lewes
		Eastbourne
		Bexhill & Battle
		Wealden
		Hastings & Rye
C 41	Kent: West	Sevenoaks
		Tonbridge & Malling
		Tunbridge Wells
		Dartford
		Gravesham
		Medway
		Gillingham
		Chatham & Aylesford
		Maidstone & The Weald
		Faversham & Mid Kent
		Sittingbourne & Sheppey
C 42	Kent: East	Ashford
		Canterbury
		Folkestone & Hythe
		Dover
		Thanet South
		Thanet North
C 38	Surrey	Spelthorne
		Esher & Walton
		Runnymede & Weybridge
		Woking
		Surrey Heath
		Guildford
		Surrey South West
		Mole Valley
		Epsom & Ewell
		Surrey East
		Reigate
C 21	Buckinghamshire	Aylesbury
		Buckingham
		Chesham & Amersham
		Wycombe
		Beaconsfield
		Milton Keynes North East
		Milton Keynes South West
C 35	Berkshire	Windsor
		Slough
		Bracknell
		Maidenhead
		Newbury
		Wokingham
		Reading West
		Reading East

Top Up Area		
No	Name	Current Constituencies Included
C 18	Oxfordshire	Oxford West & Abingdon
		Oxford East
		Henley
		Wantage
		Banbury
		Witney

LONDON

L 3	North Central London	Kensington & Chelsea
		Hammersmith & Fulham
		Cities of London & Westminster
		Regent's Park & Kensington North
		Holborn & St Pancras
		Hampstead & Highgate
		Islington South & Finsbury
		Islington North
		Hackney South & Shoreditch
		Hackney North & Stoke Newington
		Bethnal Green & Bow
L 4	North East London	Poplar & Canning Town
		West Ham
		East Ham
		Barking
		Hornchurch
		Dagenham
		Romford
		Upminster
		Ilford North
		Ilford South
L 2	North London	Chingford & Woodford Green
		Leyton & Wanstead
		Walthamstow
		Enfield, Southgate
		Enfield North
		Edmonton
		Tottenham
		Hornsey & Wood Green
		Finchley & Golders Green
		Hendon
		Chipping Barnet
L 1	North West London	Harrow West
		Harrow East
		Brent North
		Brent South
		Brent East
		Hayes & Harlington
		Uxbridge
		Ruislip – Northwood
		Ealing North
		Ealing, Acton & Shepherd's Bush
		Ealing Southall
L 6	South Central London	Battersea
		Putney
		Tooting
		Streatham
		Dulwich & West Norwood
		Camberwell & Peckham
		Lewisham West
		Lewisham, Deptford
		Lewisham East
		Vauxhall
		Southwark North & Bermondsey

Top Up Area		
No	**Name**	**Current Constituencies Included**
L 5	South West London	Feltham & Heston
		Brentford & Isleworth
		Wimbledon
		Mitcham & Morden
		Kingston & Surbiton
		Richmond Park
		Twickenham
		Sutton & Cheam
		Carshalton & Wallington
L 7	South East London	Croydon South
		Croydon Central
		Croydon North
		Greenwich & Woolwich
		Erith & Thamesmead
		Old Bexley & Sidcup
		Bexleyheath & Crayford
		Beckenham
		Orpington
		Bromley & Chislehurst
		Eltham

SOUTH WEST

No	Name	Current Constituencies Included
C 29	Cornwall	Falmouth & Camborne
		St Ives
		Truro & St Austell
		Cornwall North
		Cornwall South East
C 30	Devon	Plymouth, Sutton
		Plymouth, Devonport
		Torbay
		Teignbridge
		Devon East
		Exeter
		Devon West and Torridge
		Tiverton & Honiton
		Devon North
		Totnes
		Devon South West
C 31	Somerset	Taunton
		Bridgwater
		Yeovil
		Somerton & Frome
		Wells
C 32	Bristol and Bath	Bath
		Wansdyke
		Weston-Super-Mare
		Woodspring
		Bristol West
		Bristol North West
		Bristol East
		Bristol South
		Northavon
		Kingswood
C 17	Gloucestershire	Cheltenham
		Cotswold
		Tewkesbury
		Forest of Dean
		Gloucester
		Stroud

Top Up Area			
No	Name		Current Constituencies Included
C 33	Wiltshire		Swindon North
			Swindon South
			Wiltshire North
			Devizes
			Westbury
			Salisbury
C 34	Dorset		Christchurch
			Dorset North
			Dorset West
			Dorset South
			Poole
			Dorset Mid & North Poole
			Bournemouth East
			Bournemouth West

SCOTLAND

S 8	Scotland South		Dumfries
			Galloway & Upper Nithsdale
			Tweedale, Ettrick & Lauderdale
			Roxburgh & Berwickshire
			East Lothian
			Ayr
			Cunningham South
			Clydesdale
			Carrick, Cumnock & Doon Valley
S 1	Scotland Highlands		Caithness, Sutherland and Easter Ross
			Orkney & Shetland
			Ross, Skye & Inverness West
			Western Isles
			Argyll & Bute
			Inverness East, Nairn & Lochaber
			Moray
S 2	Scotland North East		Banff & Buchan
			Gordon
			Aberdeen Central
			Aberdeen North
			Aberdeen South
			Aberdeenshire West & Kincardine
			Dundee West
			Dundee East
			Angus
S 3	Scotland Mid and Fife		Perth
			Tayside North
			Stirling
			Ochil
			Fife Central
			Fife North East
			Kirkaldy
			Dunfermline West
			Dunfermline East
S 6	Scotland Central		Falkirk West
			Falkirk East
			Coatbridge & Chryston
			Cumbernauld & Kilsyth
			Motherwell & Wishaw
			Airdrie & Shotts
			Hamilton South
			Hamilton North and Bellshill
			East Kilbride
			Kilmarnock & Loudoun

Top Up Area			
No	**Name**		**Current Constituencies Included**
S 4	Scotland West		Cunninghame North
			Greenock & Inverclyde
			Dunbarton
			Renfrewshire West
			Strathkelvin and Bearsden
			Clydebank & Milngavie
			Paisley North
			Paisley South
			Eastwood
S 7	Lothians		Edinburgh West
			Edinburgh Pentlands
			Midlothian
			Edinburgh Central
			Edinburgh South
			Edinburgh North & Leith
			Edinburgh East & Musselburgh
			Linlithgow
			Livingstone
S 5	Glasgow		Glasgow Govan
			Glasgow Pollok
			Glasgow Maryhill
			Glasgow Springburn
			Glasgow Anniesland
			Glasgow Kelvin
			Glasgow Cathcart
			Glasgow Rutherglen
			Glasgow Shettleston
			Glasgow Baillieston
	WALES		
W 1	Wales North		Caernarfon
			Conwy
			Ynys Mon
			Wrexham
			Alyn & Deeside
			Vale of Clwyd
			Delyn
			Clwyd South
			Clwyd West
W 2	Wales Mid		Ceredigion
			Meirionnydd Nant Conwy
			Brecon & Radnorshire
			Montgomeryshire
			Carmarthen West & South Pembrokeshire
			Preseli Pembrokeshire
			Llanelli
			Carmarthen East & Dinefwr
W 3	South Wales West		Swansea West
			Swansea East
			Gower
			Neath
			Aberavon
			Bridgend
			Ogmore
W 4	South Wales Central		Cynon Valley
			Rhondda
			Pontypridd
			Vale of Glamorgan
			Cardiff North
			Cardiff West
			Cardiff South & Penarth
			Cardiff Central

| Top Up Area | | Current Constituencies Included |
No	Name	
W 5	South Wales East	Caerphilly
		Merthyr Tydfil & Rhymney
		Blaenau Gwent
		Islwyn
		Torfaen
		Monmouth
		Newport West
		Newport East
	NORTHERN IRELAND	
N 1	Northern Ireland East	Belfast North
		Belfast South
		Belfast East
		Belfast West
		Antrim North
		Antrim South
		Antrim East
		Lagan Valley
		Strangford
		Down North
N 2	Northern Ireland West	Upper Bann
		Fermanagh and South Tyrone
		Newry and Armagh
		Down South
		Foyle
		Londonderry East
		Mid Ulster
		West Tyrone

Method of Working

One of the first decisions was to pursue our work in an open manner inviting representations from the public. The reason behind this was twofold. We wanted to capture the widest possible range of views and opinions on the important issue under our scrutiny - to involve the public as well as those with a direct interest in electoral reform. And second, although broadly familiar with the issues, we needed quickly to build our knowledge and understanding of voting systems through ready access to information, individuals and institutions with an interest in electoral matters.

2.   In considering how to conduct our analysis of the various alternative systems we decided that it was essential not only to test possible alternatives against the criteria set down in our terms of reference, but also to test them against the existing system - in effect using FPTP as the benchmark. This approach enabled us systematically to test possible alternatives not only against the weaknesses of FPTP but, as importantly, also against its considerable strengths. We believe that this improved significantly the prospects of the Commission recommending an alternative that is genuinely and demonstrably the best alternative to the existing system.

3.   We decided against inviting written evidence directly from any particular individuals or organisations in favour of an open invitation to the public. We also decided against holding formal oral evidence- taking sessions which would have been incompatible with a report this autumn. Instead, we took ourselves to the main centres of population throughout the country and held 'hearings' for anyone who wished to come. These are described in more detail below.

Written Evidence

4.   Written submissions to the Commission were invited through a series of advertisements in the national and regional press in the week beginning 2nd February 1998. These included, in no particular order, The Times, The Daily Telegraph, The Guardian, The Independent, The Mail, The Express, The Sun, The Western Mail, The Scotsman, The (Glasgow) Herald, The Belfast Telegraph, The Irish News and The Belfast Newsletter. These advertisements provided details of the Commission's membership, terms of reference, and postal and e-mail addresses. At the time of publication we had received in the more than 1,500 written submissions, from members of the public, academics, political parties, Members of Parliament and various lobby groups.

Regional Meetings

5.   The Commission held the following series of nine public meetings at national and regional capitals across the UK between March and July 1998:

- **Cardiff,** 10 March
- **Belfast,** 12 March
- **Edinburgh,** 24 March
- **Leeds,** 6 April
- **Manchester,** 21 April

- **Birmingham,** 28 April
- **Plymouth,** 29 April
- **Newcastle,** 5 May
- **London,** Church House, Westminster,1 July

6.   A wide range of individuals and groups received either personal invitations to or general notification of the meetings. These included, in most instances, local MPs, local government representatives, various community and interest groups, local business and trade union representatives and academics. Notification to the wider public was by means of advertisements in local newspapers and a poster campaign in local libraries, schools, citizen's advice bureaux and other public buildings. In addition members of the Commission gave interviews to the press and local media in the days preceding the meetings. Turnout at the meetings varied ranging from 10 in Belfast to 125 in Manchester and Birmingham and around 300 in London. A total of about 1,000 people attended. Around 300 contributed to the discussion.

7.   We believe that the public meetings contributed significantly to our work They confirmed the existence of a rich vein of strongly held and confidently expressed views on electoral reform and related matters, which we found usefully informative. We would not, however, claim that the views expressed during these meetings were broadly representative of the British public as a whole. Those who contributed were in the main actively involved with electoral reform or local politics and, more often than not, supporting a particular system, including some keen advocates of the FPTP status quo.

8.   However, a number of important themes did emerge from these meetings which have featured in our thinking and our subsequent recommendations. These include a widely expressed desire for a more consensual and less confrontational democracy, a strong opposition to increasing the power of political parties in the electoral process, and a powerful surge of support for a well planned and funded civic education campaign in the run up to the referendum.

Further Testing Public Opinion

9.   The regional meetings enabled us to explore the views of particular groups within the community, but were not, as we have explained above, an adequate test of public opinion generally. We therefore invited NOP to undertake a number of focus groups on our behalf to test public views on a range of issues relating to electoral systems. NOP's report is published in Volume 2 of this report.

10.   We are grateful to Charter 88 for inviting us to attend meetings with groups representing the young and ethnic minorities. These meeting took place on 20 April and 11 May respectively. Members of the Commission attended a number of other meetings to which they were invited.

Seeking the Views of Academic Political Scientists

11.   The relevant academic world responded with enthusiasm to the Commission's call for written submissions. All of these submissions informed our thinking and were immensely helpful in guiding us through the miscellany of systems and hybrid system under our scrutiny. In addition we invited David Butler to chair a group of eminent psephologists in an attempt to provide agreed answers to a number of technical questions about the qualities of certain systems. We are particularly grateful to David Butler and his colleagues for their efforts on our behalf. To have a produced a consensus report on technical issues (not recommendations) where academics traditionally disagree is an impressive achievement. The report is published in Volume 2 of this report.

Obtaining the Views of Members of Parliament

12.   The Commission invited all Members of Parliament to attend an open meeting in the Grand Committee Room of the House of Commons on Tuesday 30 June. Well over 100 MPs attended what proved to be a lively and informative meeting. Some Members of the Commission also attended a meeting of the All Party Group on Electoral Reform. It was, of course, open to any MP to submit written evidence to the Commission.

Examining Electoral Systems Overseas

13.   We felt strongly that in order confidently to recommend an alternative to the existing electoral system, we needed to see and understand at first hand the practical impact and limitations of various electoral systems in comparable countries overseas. To this end the Commission undertook fact-finding visits to the Republic of Ireland on 20-21 May 1998 and Germany on 15-16 June 1998. Three members of the Commission travelled to New Zealand and Australia between 25 May and 4 June 1998. In the course of these visits we had access to a wide range of senior politicians (retired and active), academics, officials and political journalists. A full list of our interlocutors is at Annex F.

14.   How well these countries fare under their respective systems and what we have been able to learn from them is addressed in Chapter Four of this report. Apart from New Zealand where the recent transition to MMP has raised public and media interest in electoral systems and their impact on the culture and effectiveness of government, the electoral systems were simply not in dispute. The Additional Member System has become a well established and fully accepted feature of the German democratic process. There is no serious pressure for the change from the public or politicians. Equally in Australia, the electoral systems, AV for the House of Representatives and STV for the Senate, on the whole work well and are widely supported. Similarly in Ireland STV has been operation since the 1920s and is still widely popular with the public if less certainly with the majority of politicians.

15.   But three main conclusions emerged from these visits:

- The first and possibly the most important was that electoral systems can operate in very different ways in different countries. Considerable caution is needed when reading across international experience. The fact that certain countries share democratic principles, ancestry, language or culture is not sufficient to guarantee that a system will operate in the same way in each of them.

- The second was the importance of building in a review process not only to monitor the impact of any new system, but to have on-going responsibility for oversight of elections and electoral matters generally. These functions are carried out by independent electoral commissions in Australia and New Zealand.

- Third the need for a well-planned and publicly-funded civic education programme in the run up to the referendum.

Access to Submissions received by the Commission

16.   The Commission wishes the evidence it has received in the course of its work to be available for scrutiny. Items of key evidence received by the Commission are being published in Volume 2 of this report which is available as a CD-Rom and on the Internet. The website number is http://www.official-documents.co.uk/document/cm40/4090/4090.htm. We have arranged for copies of this evidence also to be placed in the House of Commons and House of Lords Libraries. Public access will also be available through the Public Record Office soon after the date of publication.

Sources of data

17.   The projections of outcomes for elections under the system recommended by the Commission, which are at paragraphs 155 and 157 and Annex B of this report, are based upon analyses conducted on behalf of the Commission by Professor Patrick Dunleavy of the London School of Economics and Dr Helen Margetts of Birkbeck College. It should be noted that these projections superimposed voting patterns from both 1992 and 1997 onto the scheme proposed by the Commission and consequently projections for both elections assume a House of Commons of 659 Members. The figures relating to outcomes under AV, contained in paragraph 82 and 83, derive from projections made by Professor John Curtice and from Professor Dunleavy and Dr Margetts' work published in the volume 'Making Votes Count'. We are also grateful to Professor Dunleavy for the map at Annex C of this report and to Professor Ron Johnston of the University of Bristol for his kind permission to reproduce the graph demonstrating the changing pattern of bias.

List of International Interlocutors

IRELAND

Conor Brady – Editor of the Irish Times

John Bruton TD – Leader of Fine Gael and former Taosieach

Davd Byrne – Attorney General

Denis Coghlan – Irish Times

Stephen Collins – Sunday Times

Noel Dempsey TD – Minister for the Environment and Local Government

Jim Downey – Irish Independent

Professor Ronan Fanning – University College Dublin

Jimmy Farrelly – Secretary General of the Department of the Environment

Dr Fergus Finlay – Journalist

Dr Garret Fitzgerald TD – former Taoiseach and academic

Dr Michael Gallagher – Trinity College Dublin

Professor Gerard Hogan – Trinity College Dublin

Brendan Howlin TD – Deputy Leader of the Labour Party

Geraldine Kennedy – Irish Times

Professor Joe Lee – University College Cork

Michael McDowell – Barrister

Jim O'Donnell – Secretary, Oireachtas Committee on the Constitution

Ruairi Quinn TD – Leader of the Labour Party

Pat Rabbitte TD – Democratic Left

John Rogers – Senior Council

Dr Richard Sinnott – University College Dublin

Brendan Walsh – Sheriff of Dublin

Dr T K Whittaker – Retired Cabinet Secretary

NEW ZEALAND

Jim Anderton, Leader of the Alliance

John Armstrong, Political editor, NZ Herald

Simon Arnold, Special Adviser to the Prime Minister, former CEO Manufacturers' Federation

Rick Barber, Labour MP

Tim Barnett, Labour MP

Jonathan Boston, Victoria University

Laurie Bryant, worked on publicity campaigns prior to 1992 and 1993 referenda

Mark Burton MP, Labour Chief Whip

Rt Hon Helen Clark MP, Leader of the Labor Party

Hon Wyatt Creech, Leader of the House and Deputy Leader of the National Party

Dr Michael Cullen MP, Deputy Leader of the Labor Party

Hon John Delamere, Minister for Customs, Associate Treasurer, Associate Minister of Health and NZ First Maori MP

Rod Donald, Alliance MP, Leader of Greens, member of Electoral Reform Coalition and Electoral Law Committee

Hon Peter Dunne, Leader of United Party and sole United MP

Brent Edwards, Political Editor, Evening Post

Alan Emerson, Communications Trumps (political lobbyists)

Angela Foulkes, Secretary, New Zealand Council of Trade Unions

Dr Bryan Gould, Vice-Chancellor, Waikato University

Dr Paul Harris, Chief Executive of the New Zealand Electoral Commission

Marie Hasler, National MP (Chair)

Michael Hirschfeld, Labour Party President

Pete Hodgson, Labour MP and Deputy Chair, Electoral Law Committee

Graham Hunt, Journalist and author of "Why MMP must Go'

Rt Hon Jonathon Hunt MP, Shadow Leader of the House

Professor Keith Jackson (by phone), Emeritus Professor in Politics, Canterbury University, Christchurch

Colin James, author and senior political journalist

Colin Keating, Secretary for Justice and Electoral Commissioner

Sir Kenneth Keith, Court of Appeal Judge, member of Royal Commission on the Voting System

Hon Doug Kidd, Speaker

Rt Hon David Lange, NZ Prime Minister (1984 – 1989)

Stephen Levine, Victoria University

Peter Luke, Political Editor, the Press

Victoria Main, Political Editor, Dominion

Ron Mark MP, NZ First MP and Chief Whip

Matt McCarten, Alliance Chairman

Dave McGee, Clerk of the House and Member of the Independent Panel which oversaw the education campaign prior to the referenda

Rt Hon Ian McKay, President of the Electoral Commission

Dr Raymond Miller, Helena Katt and Peter Aimer – Department of Political Studies at
Auckland University

Al Morrison, Political Editor, Radio New Zealand

Mark Prebble, Adviser in Prime Ministers Department

Hon Richard Prebble, Leader of ACT

Ian Rewell, Deputy Speaker

Nigel Roberts, Victoria University

Bernard Robertson, Editor, New Zealand Law Journal

Marie Schroff, Cabinet Secretary

Ken Shirley, ACT MP

Bob Simcock, National MP

John Slater, Businessman and Chairman, Northern Division of National Party (since August
1998 Chair of the National Party)

Hon Nick Smith, Minister for Conservation

Tony Steel, National MP

Maryan Street, Labour Party President from 1994-96, now Director of Labour
Studies, Auckland University

Ross Tanner, Deputy State Services Commissioner

Geoff Thompson, National Party President

Mark Unsworth, Saunders and Unsworth, political lobbyists

The Hon Justice John Wallace, Former Chair of the Royal Commission on the Electoral System

Don Walter, Chairman, Anglian Water International

Phil Whelan, Chief Electoral Officer

Pansy Wong and Arthur Anse (National list MPs)

Doug Woolerton, NZ First MP

AUSTRALIA

Sir John Carrick KCMG

Rob Chalmers, Inside Canberra

Lynton Crosby, Federal Director, Liberal Party of Australia

Senator The Hon John Faulkner – Labor Senator and Leader of the Opposition and former Minister

Petro Georgiou, MP Liberal Member for Kooyong and former special adviser to PM Fraser

Gary Gray, Labor Party National Secretary

Bill Gray – Australian Electoral Commissioner

The Rt Hon R J L Hawke – Labor Prime Minister 1983-1991

Gerard Henderson, Executive Director of the Sydney Institute

Philip Higginson, Federal President, Australia-Britain Chamber of Commerce

Senator The Hon Robert Hill, Liberal Senator for South Australia – Minister for the Environment and Leader of the Government in the Senate

Professor Colin Hughes, former Electoral Commissioner and professor of political science

Professor Malcolm MacKerras, Professor of Politics, University College, New South Wales

Michael Maley – Director of Research and International Services, Australian Electoral Commission (AEC)

Sir John Mason KCMG, former British High Commissioner to Australia

Professor Ian McAllister, Professor and Director, Research School of Social Sciences, Australian National University.

The Hon Bob McMullan MP – Labor MP and Shadow Minister for Industrial Relation, Finance and the Arts

Senator The Hon Nick Minchin, Liberal Senator and Special Minister of State assisting the Prime Minister

Michael Moore, Independent Member, ACT Legislative Assembly – Minister for Health in the current Liberal government

Professor Richard Mulgan, Senior Lecturer at Australian and commentator on MMP in NZ

Alison Purvis- acting Commissioner for the ACT Electoral Commission

Senator Robert Ray – Labor Senator and former Minister

Dennis Shanahan, Vice President Parliamentary Press Gallery

The Rt Hon Ian Sinclair MP, Speaker of the House of Representatives and National Party Member

Zeke Solomon, Partner, Allen, Allen and Hemsley

Lenore Taylor, Australia Financial Review

GERMANY

Herr Rainhard Bartella, Deutscher Staedtetag

Herr Meinrad Belle MdB (CDU)

Frau Sabine Berthold, Bundeszentrale fuer politische Bildung

Herr Friedrich Bohl MdB (CDU), Minister of State, Federal Chancellary

Herr Wolfgang Bosbach MdB (CDU)

Herr Hartmut Buettner MdB (CDU), Vice-Chairman of the Bundestag Internal Affairs Committee

Herr Gerald Haefner MdB (Green Party)

Herr Johann Hahlen, Federal Returning Officer

Herr Fritz-Rudolf Koerper MdB (SPD)

Herr Professor Martin Morlok, Director, FernUniversitat Hagen

Herr Professor Dr Karlheinz Niclauss, University of Bonn

Herr Ruprecht Polenz MdB (CDU)

Frau Cornella Rogall-Grothe, Federal Ministry of the Interior

State Secretary, Prof Dr Kurt Schelter, Federal Interior Ministry

Herr Otto Schily, MdB (SPD)

Herr Rezzo Schlauch MdB (Green Party)

Herr Andreas Schmidt MdB, CDU Whip

Herr Wilhelm Schmidt MdB, SPD Whip

Frau Ulla Schmidt MdB (SPD)

Herr Wolfgang Schmitt MdB (Green Party)

Herr Dr Schnapauff, Director General, Federal Ministry of the Interior

Herr Clemens Schwalbe MdB (CDU)

Herr Dr Hermann Otto Solms MdB, Chairman of the FDP Parliamentary Party

Herr Dr Max Stadler MdB (FDP)

Frau Dr Antje Vollmer MdB (Green Party) - Vice President of the Bundestag

Philipp Graf von Walderdorff, Deutscher Industrie and Handlestag

Herr Dr Ludolf-Georg von Wartenberg, Chief Executive of Bundesverband der Deutschen Industrie (CBI equivalent)

Herr Dieter Wiefelsputz MdB (SPD)

Frau Heide Wright MdB (SPD)

Acknowledgements

Listed below are those political parties, Members of Parliament, policy groups, representative and campaigning organizations, academics and other experts from whom the Commission has received submissions. The Commission would also like to thank those members of the general public, too numerous to list in full here, who also submitted views and contributions.

Dr Mark Aspinwall, University of Durham

The Association of Electoral Administrators

Tony Baldry MP

Professor Vernon Bogdanor, Oxford University

Dr Stephen Bosworth, Girne American University

Rt Hon Virginia Bottomley MP

Professor Rodney Brazier, University of Manchester

Richard Burden MP

Dale Campbell-Savours MP

The Centre for Policy Studies

Charter 88

The Conservative Party

The de Borda Institute

Democracy Design Forum

Democratic Audit

Democrats Action Group for Gaining Electoral Reform

Professor Michael Dummett, Oxford University

Professor Patrick Dunleavy, London School of Economics

The Electoral Reform Society

The Electoral Reform Society of Australia

Nigel Evans MP

Dr David Farrell, University of Manchester and Dr Michael Gallagher, Trinity College, Dublin

The Fawcett Society

George Foulkes MP

Roger Gale MP

Chistopher Gill MP

Ken Gladdish, University of Reading

Green Party

Llin Golding MP

Bruce Grocott MP

Donald Gorrie MP

Kelvin Hopkins MP

Professor Ron Johnston, University of Bristol

The Joseph Forum

The Labour Party

Labour Campaign for Electoral Reform

Tom Levitt MP

The Liberal Party

The Liberal Democrats

Martin Linton MP

Professor Iain McLean, Oxford University

Peter Kellner

Petr Kopecky, University of Sheffield

Barbara Lindsay, Manchester Metropolitan University

Professor Joni Lovenduski, Southampton University and Dr Pippa Norris, Joan Shorenstein
Centre on the Press, Politics and Public Policy

Dr Helen Margetts, Birkbeck College

Dr Edmund Marshall, University of Bradford

Austin Mitchell MP

Rhodri Morgan MP

Professor Philip Norton, University of Hull

Northern Ireland Forum for Political Dialogue

Professor Brendan O'Leary, London School of Economics

Peter Pike MP

Professor Richard Rose, University of Strathclyde

Andrew Rowe MP

Dr Edward Royle, University of York

Martin Salter MP and Jonathan Shaw MP

Select Your Member Voting Society

Barry Sheerman MP

Scottish National Party

Socialist Movement

Phyllis Starkey MP

Gisela Stuart MP

Tory Reform Group

Sir Teddy Taylor MP

Gareth Thomas MP

Welsh Labour Action

Select Bibliography

Bale, T. and Kopecky, P., "Can Young Pups Teach an Old Dog New Tricks? Lessons for British Reformers from Eastern Europe's New Constitutional Democracies", *The Journal of Legislative Studies,* 1998

Blackburn, R., *The Electoral System in Britain* (Macmillan 1995)

Boundary Commission Fourth Periodical Report (HMSO 1995)

Bogdanor V., *Power and the People: a Guide to Constitutional Reform* (Gollancz 1997)

Bogdanor V., *What is Proportional Representation* (Martin Robertson 1984)

Butler D., *The Case for an Electoral Commission* (The Hansard Society 1998)

Butler, D. and Kavanagh, D., *The British General Election of 1997* (Macmillan 1997)

The Constitution Unit, *Elections Under Regional Lists* (The Constitution Unit 1998)

The Constitution Unit, *Report of the Commission on the Conduct of Referendums* (The Constitution Unit 1996)

Curtice, J. and Steed, M., *Proportionality and exaggeration in the British electoral system,* Electoral Studies, Volume 5, 1983.

Dummett, M., *Principles of Electoral Reform* (Oxford 1997)

Dunleavy, P., Hix, S. and Margetts, H., *Counting on Europe: Proportional Representation and the June 1999 Elections to the European Parliament* (LSE Public Policy Group 1998)

Dunleavy, P., Margetts, H. and Weir, S., *The Other National Lottery: Misrepresentation and malapportionment in British elections* (Charter 88 1996)

Dunleavy, P., Margetts, H. and Weir, S., *Making Votes Count and Making Votes Count 2* (Democratic Audit 1998)

Farrell, D., *Comparing Electoral Systems* (Prentice Hall/Harvester Wheatsheaf 1997)

Hansard Society, *Report of the Hansard Society Commission on Electoral Reform* (Hansard Society 1976, republished 1998)

Hart, J., *Proportional Representation: Critics of the British Electoral System 1820-1945* (Clarendon 1992)

Jeffery, C., "Electoral Reform: Learning from Germany", *The Political Quarterly,* 1998

Johnston, R.J., "Proportional Representation and a 'Fair Electoral System' for the United Kingdom", *The Journal of Legislative Studies,* 1998

Johnston, R.J., Pattie, C. and Rossiter, D., "Defining constituencies for proportional representation", *Renewal,* 1998

Linton, M. and Southcott, M., *Making Votes Count: the Case for Electoral Reform* (Profile Books 1998)

Linton, M. and ed. Georghiou, M., *Labour's Road to Electoral Reform* (Labour Campaign for Electoral Reform 1993)

Maclean, I. and Butler, D. (ed), *Fixing the Boundaries: Defining and Redefining Single Member Electoral Districts* (Dartmouth 1996)

Norris, P. and Gavin, N. (ed), *Britain Votes 1997* (Oxford University Press1997)

The Plant Report, *Democracy, Representation and Elections,* Report of the Working Party on Elections (Labour Party 1993)

Representation: Journal of Representative Democracy (McDougall Trust 1995 onwards)

Reynolds, A. and Reilly, B. (ed), *The International IDEA Handbook of Electoral System Design,* (International Institute for Democracy an Electoral Assistance 1997)

Roberts G.K., "Neglected aspects of the German electoral system", *Representation,* 1997

Smyth, G. (ed), *Refreshing the Parts: Electoral Reform and British Politics* (Lawrence and Wishart 1992)

Towards a Better Democracy: Report of the Royal Commission on the Electoral System (New Zealand Electoral Commission 1986)

Voting Under MMP (New Zealand Electoral Commission 1996)

Watts, D., *Electoral Reform: Achieving a Sense of Proportion* (PAVIC Publications, Sheffield Hallam University 1994

Printed in the UK for The Stationery Office Limited on behalf of the
Controller of Her Majesty's Stationery Office
Dd 5068378   10/98   65536   Job No 62727   42/44514